I0152083

HOLY ABORTION?

A Theological Critique of the
Religious Coalition for Reproductive Choice

Why Christians and Christian Churches
Should Reconsider the Issue of Abortion

Michael J. Gorman
and
Ann Loar Brooks

Wipf and Stock Publishers
Eugene, Oregon

Wipf and Stock Publishers
199 West 8th Avenue, Suite 3
Eugene, Oregon 97401

Holy Abortion?
A Theological Critique of the
Religious Coalition for Reproductive Choice
By Michael J. Gorman and Ann Loar Brooks

A Project of the National Pro-life Religious Council
Copyright © 2003, by Michael J. Gorman and Ann Loar Brooks
ISBN: 1-59244-185-8
Publication Date: April 2003

MORE ADVANCE PRAISE FOR *HOLY ABORTION?*
(continued from the back cover)

"A powerful statement on the immorality of abortion on demand that should be taken seriously by all churches."

> — *Donald G. Bloesch*
> Emeritus Professor of Theology
> University of Dubuque Theological Seminary

"Michael Gorman and Ann Brooks have done the mainline denominations a great service in unmasking the sub-Christian rhetoric of self-idolatry promoted by the literature of the Religious Coalition for Reproductive Choice. Every mainline denomination associated with RCRC should now rethink such an association."

> — *Robert Gagnon*
> Associate Professor of New Testament
> Pittsburgh Theological Seminary

"On the most intensely controverted question in our public life, this book may not move people from the pro-choice to the pro-life column. That is not its chief purpose. Its chief purpose, as I understand it, is to make the case that religious communities should care about their own moral and spiritual integrity. *Holy Abortion?* offers convincing evidence that the Religious Coalition for Reproductive Choice advances positions that are in clear conflict with the teachings of religious communities that support the organization.

Disagreements about abortion will go on and on. Whatever our convictions on the question, we must never despair of the power of continuing conversation and persuasion. Honest conversation and persuasion begin with honesty. This little book is a simple and compelling appeal for honesty."

> — *Rev. Richard John Neuhaus*
> President, Religion and Public Life
> Editor, *First Things*

continued

"This small book makes a significant contribution in clarifying the theological and moral assumptions implicit in three major evaluations of abortion. By demonstrating how closely the positions on abortion resemble the Christian tradition's views on war, the authors offer a thoughtful and important challenge to the contemporary church."

— Christine D. Pohl
Professor of Social Ethics
Asbury Theological Seminary

"Gorman and Brooks give a brilliant account of the reversal of values regarding abortion in which vice is seen as virtue and virtue as vice, thus obscuring the deep evil of abortion and its corruptive impact on our culture."

— H. Tristram Engelhardt, Jr., Ph.D., M.D.
Professor of Philosophy, Rice University
Professor of Medicine Emeritus, Baylor College of Medicine
Co-editor, *Christian Bioethics*

About the Authors

A United Methodist layman, Michael J. Gorman is Professor of New Testament and Early Church History, as well as Dean of the Ecumenical Institute of Theology, at St. Mary's Seminary & University in Baltimore, Maryland. He is the author of the book *Abortion and the Early Church;* a co-author with Paul Stallsworth, Stanley Hauerwas, and others of *The Church and Abortion: In Search of New Ground for Response*; and the author of several articles and sermons on abortion. Dr. Gorman also serves on the Advisory Board of Lifewatch/The Taskforce of United Methodists on Abortion and Sexuality and is a participant in the international Orthodox Peace Fellowship. He is a member of the Society of Biblical Literature and the Society of Christian Ethics, and he has published articles and books in the field of biblical studies, including *Elements of Biblical Exegesis*; *Cruciformity: Paul's Narrative Spirituality of the Cross*; and the forthcoming *Apostle of the Crucified Lord: A Theological Introduction to Paul and His Letters*. He lives near Baltimore with his wife and three children.

Ann Loar Brooks is an Episcopalian laywoman with a long-standing interest in peace, justice, and life issues. She earned her M.A. in Church Ministries at the Ecumenical Institute of Theology in Baltimore, where she did research on the theological and pastoral aspects of abortion and related issues. Ms. Brooks is a trained biblical storyteller and has served several churches in various capacities. A former Wall Street banker, she is currently working on a book about a modern-day Mary Magdalene. She lives with her husband and three children in Baltimore.

Both authors wish to express their gratitude to the National Pro-life Religious Council for the invitation to write this small book, and to members of the Council who provided assistance and advice. We also wish to thank those who read and commented on drafts of all or part of the book: Rev. Phillip Brown, Ms. Georgette Forney, Prof. Stanley Hauerwas, Rev. Mr. Pat Keane, Rev. Leonard Klein, Ms. Terry Schlossberg, and Rev. Paul Stallsworth. Special thanks are also owed to Pat Keane for his research assistance. We have made every effort to be fair and accurate in our descriptions and analyses of RCRC and its affiliates. Any remaining deficiencies are in no way the responsibility of those who assisted us.

CONTENTS

IF THERE IS ANYTHING THAT RELIGION should be concerned with, it is truth. While politicians, partisans, social activists, and marketers may be willing to surrender the truth to achieve the goal, religious leaders ought to instead surrender the goal to achieve the truth. This is especially so of Christians. Our Lord said, "I am the way, the truth and the life." He often began his instruction with, "I tell you the truth...." Truth-telling is at the heart of the Gospel. The Gospel is at the heart of Truth.

In *Holy Abortion?* the authors have delivered a great gift to the religious community: the truth about religion and abortion. This treatise uncovers the dubious alliance between (on the one hand) a nearly universally suspect moral position and the groups and individuals who promote it and (on the other) the communities and organizations of truth-seekers who have wrestled with it and have even agonized over it.

Holy Abortion? is a well-documented, reasoned exposé of the Religious Coalition for Reproductive Choice (RCRC). In publishing it, the National Pro-life Religious Council (NPRC) hopes, indeed prays, that it will spark a renewed and painfully honest conversation about the never-ending question of the role of religion and religious groups in shaping society's disposition toward the most vulnerable members of the human family, the unborn, and the mothers and fathers who are inseparably linked to them.

It is our hope and prayer that this honest conversation will quickly lead to the withdrawal of religious entanglement with abortion advocacy. So-called reproductive-rights groups, abortion providers, and political organizations have their own motives, objectives, and methods for advancing the pro-choice agenda. The religious communities that hold membership or interest in RCRC do not at all share these motives, objectives, and methods.

Though NPRC endorses this book, it is the work of two individuals who have no formal affiliation with NPRC and have been given complete freedom to develop and express their own perspective. The members of the National Pro-life Religious Council urge the reader to approach this material with an open and a constructively critical mind.

Someone somewhere said, "A problem revealed is a problem half-solved." Dr. Michael Gorman and Ms. Ann Loar Brooks have accomplished the former. It is up to the rest of us to accomplish the latter.

Rev. Rob Schenck
National Pro-life Religious Council, Washington, DC

Introduction: Holy Abortion?

"Gracious Provider of Care and Protection/Bless this building and those who work here/The doctors and nurses and other health care workers/Who provide safe, legal, caring and loving reproductive health services, including abortion, to women in need/Who recognize the rights of women to make reproductive choices/*They are doing God's work*/We celebrate their concern and commitment."

— Blessing for Providers of Women's Health Care,
in RCRC's *Prayerfully Pro-Choice: Resources for Worship*, p. 101

"My commitment to choice comes from my belief that you have the right to decide whether you want to have children or not. The bottom line is that if someone does not want to have a child they should not be forced into it. That's between the woman, her man, if she chooses to make him aware, and God, whoever God is.

"I talk about God because God and I are very close. God gives you choice. *God gives you freedom of choice. That's in the Bible.*"

— Whoopi Goldberg, *The Choices We Made*,
quoted in RCRC's *Prayerfully Pro-Choice: Resources for Worship*, p. 35[1]

STANLEY HAUERWAS HAS SAID that the "moral discourse in most of our churches is but a pale reflection of what you find in *Time* magazine."[2] He may have been a bit too generous; perhaps this discourse is more a reflection of Hollywood and its icons.

One might think it unfair to focus on or criticize — or even to use — a quote from Whoopi Goldberg that appears in one printed sermon, in one publication, as representative of the position espoused by the Religious Coalition for Reproductive Choice (RCRC). But the sad fact is that her words *epitomize* RCRC's point of view.

Because both RCRC and several mainline Protestant Christian denominations support the current legal status of abortion in the United States, a superficial reading of RCRC documents and certain mainline-Protestant church documents might suggest that they are in agreement. In fact, however, they diverge dramatically at several essential points. In sum, the RCRC position proclaims, "***Abortion is holy because God is pro-choice***," while the basic mainline position proclaims, "***Abortion is tragic because God is the giver of life***." This and other fundamental differences suggest, not that RCRC and the mainline churches have a natural and logical affiliation, but that they are inappropriately joined and ought to be separated. To borrow a Pauline image, they are unequally yoked (2 Cor. 6:14), and it is time for the relationship between the mainline churches — and indeed all Christian bodies — and RCRC to end.

This book seeks, among other things, to make the case for that permanent separation. It begins with an examination of RCRC itself and then highlights six themes that run throughout RCRC's literature. These themes are then contrasted with several themes found in the official statements on abortion and sexuality of denominations that have (or, in some cases, used to have or considered having) official ties to RCRC. The contrast is so stark, it will be shown, that affiliation with RCRC is a denial of these churches' official positions. Finally, the last major section of the book seeks to advance the conversation about abortion in the Christian churches by drawing on significant theological voices that RCRC ignores.

We should quickly add, however, that this project is not merely about one organization and a handful of affiliated denominations. It is about a significant problem facing our culture and our churches, and about a spirit that permeates more than one body. Therefore, what we have to say, we hope, will be of significance beyond the specific situation we address. We intend to make a contribution to a far wider audience than one interested solely in RCRC.

I. Introducing the Religious Coalition for Reproductive Choice

RCRC's Mission Statement and Vision

THE RELIGIOUS COALITION FOR REPRODUCTIVE CHOICE (RCRC), founded in 1973 by ten denominations and faith groups as the Religious Coalition for Abortion Rights (RCAR), describes itself as "the interfaith movement for choice" and as the only national confederation of religious bodies that promotes pro-choice policies.[3] Nearly 40 national organizations from Christian and Jewish denominations, movements, and faith-based groups, as well as Unitarian, humanist, and ethical associations, now make up its membership.[4] These member bodies and many individuals support RCRC activities to preserve "reproductive choice," according to its stated mission:

> The Religious Coalition for Reproductive Choice brings the moral power of religious communities to ensure reproductive choice through education and advocacy. The Coalition seeks to give clear voice to the reproductive issues of people of color, those living in poverty, and other underserved populations.[5]

As we will see below, one of the "underserved populations" to which RCRC devotes special attention is youth.

RCRC's basic message in its educational and advocacy work is that "the vast majority of Americans believe abortion is a complex issue that is best decided by a woman, her doctor, her family, and her God" — sometimes shortened to "a woman and her God."[6] RCRC mottos include phrases like "Pro-Faith, Pro-Family, Pro-Choice"; "We are pro-choice because of our faith"; and "Prayerfully Pro-Choice." Or, in summary: "Abortion can be a moral, ethical, and religiously responsible decision."[7] In addition to its focus on abortion, RCRC says that it seeks "faith-based solutions" to issues of sexuality, reproduction, and health care.[8]

As we will see in more detail below, RCRC actually consists of two legal entities. There is a 501(c)(4) public-policy and advocacy organization, the Religious Coalition for Reproductive Choice, Inc. (RCRC, Inc.), to which contributions are not tax-deductible. There is also an educational wing, the Religious Coalition for Reproductive Choice Educational Fund (RCRCEF), which is a 501(c)(3) organization, to which contributions are tax-deductible according to IRS regulations.

RCRC sees itself not merely as a coalition of religious organizations and individuals, but as an organization with a divine calling and mission. Its current President and CEO, Rev. Carlton W. Veazey, who is a minister of the National Baptist Convention U.S.A., speaks for many in RCRC when he says that the Coalition "has a special call" and thanks its supporters for "keeping the faith for choice."[9] Furthermore, as we will see below, RCRC views the providing of abortion services, like the choosing of abortion itself, as a sacred act.

The Major Activities of RCRC

RCRC is an active and growing organization that appears to be expanding its mission even though some Christian denominations have severed ties with it.[10] RCRC's main efforts include:[11]

- articulating a "theology of choice" to inform and guide individuals, faith communities, politicians, and the media;
- promoting safe, legal, and affordable abortion services and supporting abortion clinics;
- lobbying local, state, and national legislative bodies for ongoing legal protection of abortion rights and unfettered access to abortion and other reproductive services;
- promoting family planning services and contraception, adoption services, and affordable child care and health care;
- promoting "comprehensive sexuality education" in faith communities and schools;
- mobilizing the "grassroots" to support choice;
- mobilizing clergy to advocate for abortion in their congregations, communities, and local governments;
- "broadening the movement" to focus on black and Latino churches and on youth;
- encouraging RCRC affiliates to stimulate local faith groups to support abortion causes; and
- proclaiming to the media that RCRC's views indicate broad-based religious support of abortion.

RCRC operates primarily out of state-affiliate groups in 22 locations throughout the country. (States include California [two groups], Colorado, Florida, Illinois, Iowa, Kentucky, Maryland, Massachusetts, Michigan, Minnesota, Missouri, Nebraska, New Jersey, New Mexico, New York [three groups], Ohio, Oklahoma, Oregon, and Washington.) These affiliates offer what they refer to as "All Options" reproductive counseling services by clergy, provide pro-abortion speakers, and lobby legislative representatives.

RCRC also functions through focused networks and initiatives, ranging from services for clergy to programs targeted to specific ethnic-

and/or age-groups. As we will see below, RCRC has recently developed particular interests in educating African Americans, Latinos, young adults and teens, and even children. The following excerpt is from a sermon recommended as appropriate for children:

> Sometimes a baby starts growing in a woman's body when she doesn't want to be a mother. Maybe she is alone and doesn't have enough friends and family to help her be a good parent.... What can she do?... [T]he woman might... decide she is able to give a baby what it needs; or maybe she will choose to finish growing the baby in her body and then let another family adopt her or him. But maybe the woman won't decide either of these things. *In our country, we have a law that says a pregnant woman who doesn't want to be a mother can go to a doctor and have that doctor take the growing seed out of her body.* That's called an abortion. Life is very precious.... For many people, it is a very sad decision. But it's also very sad when babies are born to parents who can't give them the things and the love that will help them grow up healthy and happy.[12]

How and why did this organization get started? How has it evolved into the multi-tasking entity it is today?

A Brief History of RCAR/RCRC

In 1967, the Rev. Howard Moody of New York, ordained in both the American Baptist Church and the United Church of Christ, started the Clergy Consultation Service on Abortion. The Clergy Consultation Service was a network of ministers and rabbis willing to help women seeking abortions receive their desired medical services from trained professionals. At the same time, in the late 1960s and early 1970s, several mainline Protestant denominations, as well as certain Jewish groups, issued statements advocating the liberalization or elimination of abortion laws.[13] After the historic Supreme Court ruling *Roe v. Wade* in January of 1973, the fusion of these two interests — clergy support for the provision of abortion and denominational advocacy for its legalization — generated the Religious Coalition for Abortion Rights (RCAR).[14]

Beginnings
The early members of RCAR (usually represented by their social-action divisions) included conservative and reform Jewish organizations; Unitarian Universalist and humanist bodies; and, of course, mainline

Protestant churches: the American Baptist Churches, the Episcopal Church, the Christian Church (Disciples of Christ), the Presbyterian Church in the U.S. and the United Presbyterian Church (which later merged to form the Presbyterian Church (U.S.A.)), the United Church of Christ, and the United Methodist Church.[15] From the beginning, RCAR had an especially close relationship with divisions of the United Methodist Church, from which it leased office space in the United Methodist Building, across from the Supreme Court, until the end of 1993.[16]

RCAR's mission, which it expected to be a short-term project, was to proclaim and protect the abortion rights given to women by *Roe*. Its organizers were especially keen to prevent constitutional amendments to overturn *Roe*, as proposed immediately by the Roman Catholic Church and by the newly formed National Right to Life Committee.[17] The themes of religious liberty and women's rights, as arguments for access to abortion, pervaded RCAR's message from the start.[18]

RCAR began to lobby Congress regarding many abortion-related issues as they arose. For example, among the most significant issues debated in the mid-1970s was the question of the humanity or personhood of the fetus. Testifying on RCAR's behalf, Rabbi Balfour Brickner, then director of the Commission on Interfaith Activities of the American Hebrew Congregations, told a U.S. Senate subcommittee that "in Judaism the fetus in the womb was not considered a person and had 'no juridical personality of its own.' In fact, according to Brickner, a fetus did not acquire legal standing until thirty days after its birth."[19] Protestants active in RCAR agreed that a consensus did not exist, and a key plank in the organization's platform was the claim that any legislation asserting the personhood of the fetus would be tantamount to the unconstitutional establishment of religion.[20]

In the mid-1980s, RCAR began to focus on the role of women of color in the abortion arena and increased its legislative lobbying efforts. The number of RCAR lobbyists and especially activists increased exponentially in that decade.[21] Primarily, the fight was against the Hyde Amendment, which was perceived by RCAR as limiting abortion rights for women of color by restricting Medicaid funding for abortion. In addition, RCAR joined forces with the National Organization of Women (NOW) to lead pro-choice rallies in the nation's capital. The key RCAR theme of the 1980s was the affirmation of women as moral decision-makers and of abortion as a moral choice. This theme appealed especially to some (previously unreached) evangelical audiences.[22]

New Name, New Initiatives

In 1993, RCAR "expanded and accelerated our work to include the entire range of reproductive options, changed our name to the Religious Coalition for Reproductive Choice, and *renewed our struggle against the increasingly dangerous forces of religious extremism.*"[23]

The Black Church Initiative (BCI), begun in 1997, is RCRC's effort to educate African-American religious communities about abortion and sexuality. It is an extension of commitments already evident in RCRC's Women of Color Partnership, which in 1996 had published a brochure entitled "Black Ministers Support your Right to Choose." A large donation from the Ford Foundation in 2000 enabled RCRC to work toward shedding "its image as a coalition of primarily liberal white Protestants"[24] by advocating acceptance of sexuality options (including homosexual and bisexual behavior) and "safe sex" education programs within the black church. RCRC employed these funds to host the National Black Religious Summit on Sexuality in July 2000. Among the speakers at this summit was former Surgeon General Joycelyn Elders, who said at the conference that condoms may break, "but I can assure you, the vows of abstinence break far more easily than any condom."[25] A parallel "Iniciativa Latina" ("Latina/Hispanic Initiative") has now been started.

In 2000, RCRC launched the Youth Organizing Initiative (YOI) to encourage youth to generate support for abortion among their peers. In the same year, RCRC discovered via a national poll that most religious Americans do not believe that their own religion supports abortion.[26] The formation of the Youth Organizing Initiative is one of several means by which RCRC hopes to recast these beliefs.

The Youth Organizing Initiative led to the formation, in 2001, of a youth network called Spiritual Youth for Reproductive Freedom (SYRF). SYRF is aimed at people ages 16-30 who are "young, spiritual, and pro-choice" and thus are committed to maintaining "liberty, justice, and choice" in opposition to the "narrow anti-choice views of the Religious Wrong."[27] It has its own extensive web site, including a "pro-choice, pro-faith" virtual "Spirituality House," imitating a campus ministry center.[28]

Additionally, RCRC established a new advertising campaign that coincided with YOI's start-up. Its message was: "Abortion is a personal decision best left in the hands of a woman and her God."[29] This campaign would appear to appeal especially to young adults struggling with their understanding of God, religion, and sexual morality.

At the same time, RCRC publicly backed partial-birth abortion and U.S. approval of mifepristone (RU-486), the "early-abortion pill," proudly claiming to be the only faith-based group in the U.S. to do so.[30]

RCRC's interests in the black churches and in the youth population have merged in several ways. "Keeping It Real!" is a Christian sexuality-education curriculum for African-American youth ages 13 to 17. Developed by the Black Church Initiative, "Keeping It Real!" is billed as a curriculum that prepares youth to "make healthy, responsible decisions as spiritual and sexual beings."[31] The seven-week curriculum of facilitated dialogue and activities is touted as one of the first organized efforts in African-American faith communities to address sex and sexuality in both a biblical and a societal context. It is claimed that African-American clergy and lay youth educators now have a model to break the silence about sex and sexuality and begin an open dialogue with youth.

Since 1996, RCRC has campaigned against legislative attempts to limit partial-birth abortion.[32] Other recent RCRC legislative activity has focused on opposing various acts that might imply fetal personhood or restrict teenage abortion, and on supporting emergency contraception, stem-cell research, and international family-planning aid.[33] The recently inaugurated online Coalition Legislation Action Center allows RCRC supporters to contact both legislators and the media via the RCRC web site.

The RCRC of today is a mixture of old and new variations on a theme. The last few years have seen a special focus on the African-American churches and on youth. At the same time, Howard Moody's original goal of uniting pro-choice clergy remains today in RCRC's Clergy for Choice Network, a national registry of clergy from many faith traditions dedicated to preserving and promoting reproductive freedom.[34] Members pledge to support the activities to which RCRC is devoted, and especially to work for access to "safe, legal, and affordable abortion." The Network maintains a listserve (email service), and encourages clergy to participate in pro-choice counseling of pregnant women, legislative advocacy, preaching and speaking, community education, "peaceful presence" events at abortion clinics, and other activities of RCRC and its affiliates.[35]

RCRC's Literature and Online Resources

RCRC provides a vast array of printed literature and online resources to the public. This includes brochures, booklets, papers, newsletters, sexuality curricula, other printed resources, annual reports, and extensive websites.

Brochures introduce the organization and its sub-units. A quarterly newsletter called *Faith&Choices* and a special newsletter for pro-choice clergy, *Illuminata*, focus on issues, news, and RCRC projects. Other publications affirm choice, warn readers about hospital mergers that affect reproductive services, promote choice as a form of justice, contend that most Americans are pro-choice, and argue that the Bible itself, as well as both Christianity and Judaism, are pro-choice.

The main RCRC web site is found at www.rcrc.org. The website of Spiritual Youth for Reproductive Freedom is found at www.syrf.org. Each site provides numerous resources as well as links to additional pro-choice sites.

Of particular interest is RCRC's most substantive print resource, *Prayerfully Pro-Choice: Resources for Worship*. This looseleaf notebook (published ca. 2000) is available for clergy and laity who support abortion and wish to lead faith-oriented experiences and rituals that affirm these beliefs. Included in this resource are prayers, sermons and other talks, outlines of worship services, creedal statements, and other resources for faith leaders. As we will see below, this resource is an important window into the soul of RCRC.

RCRC's Funding

RCRC is funded by individuals, member organizations and affiliates (including four Christian denominations), foundations, and miscellaneous sources. It issues one annual financial report for its two quasi-divisions, the Religious Coalition for Reproductive Choice, Inc. (RCRC, Inc.), the 501(c)(4) organization that focuses on public policy and advocacy, and the Religious Coalition for Reproductive Choice Educational Fund (RCRCEF), its 501(c)(3) organization dedicated to education. In 2000, approximately 85% of RCRC's total income of $4.4-million went to RCRCEF.[36]

In 2000, all income from RCRC member organizations and affiliates supported RCRC, Inc., the public-policy arm.[37] Such support, however, was insignificant in RCRC's overall funding picture. Any change by a member organization in monetary contributions to RCRC should not be expected to have a major impact on the financial well-being of RCRC. In 2000, member organizations and affiliates contributed about $11,000 to RCRC, Inc. That amount equaled just 1.7% of the total $643,000 revenues for RCRC, Inc. (and just 0.2% of the entire organization's total revenues of $4.4-million). From the sale of contributor lists alone, RCRC, Inc. earned more than $31,000 in 2000, almost three times what member organizations and affiliates gave in hard dollars. The largest single form of RCRC, Inc.'s revenue in 2000 came from individuals — more than $600,000, or 93% of total gross income. In that year, revenues exceeded expenses by approximately $35,000, thereby eclipsing the total donations of member organizations and affiliates by almost $25,000. Had member organizations refrained from financially supporting RCRC in 2000, RCRC, Inc. would still have had a surplus in funds at the end of the fiscal year.

Clearly, RCRC does not benefit financially from its affiliation with these religious groups. The benefit must lie elsewhere.

Although member organizations do not contribute directly to RCRCEF, their membership in RCRC makes them both associates and beneficiaries of RCRCEF. RCRCEF received funding of more than $3.8-million in 2000, primarily (90%) from some 40 private foundations, each with its own agenda. For example, as noted above, in 2000 the Ford Foundation granted $350,000 to RCRCEF for the purpose of educating and "mobilizing" clergy and other religious individuals and communities about reproductive rights.[38]

Hence, while RCRC's 40 member organizations and affiliates contributed $11,000 to cover what can only be seen as a small portion of administrative costs for pro-choice advocacy, other more significant donors were funding RCRCEF to "re-educate" clergy and lay people who make up the leadership of churches and denominations, including the leadership of RCRC's affiliated denominations.

Indeed, as its mission statement declares, advocacy and education are RCRC's two primary activities. What, specifically, does RCRC teach and champion with respect to abortion? To answer this question, we turn to RCRC's own literature.

II. Examining Basic Themes in RCRC's Literature

AS WE HAVE ALREADY SEEN, RCRC maintains a large publishing operation that gets the basic themes of the organization's faith-based pro-choice message out. Of the many RCRC publications, we will pay particular attention to the collection of worship aids entitled *Prayerfully Pro-Choice: Resources for Worship*, which includes liturgical resources that "affirm reproductive choice."

We focus on *Prayerfully Pro-Choice* for two reasons, one sociological and one theological. Sociologically, when a religious organization designs and distributes thematic worship services, it is attempting to reach the masses in a religious setting and thus to have a far-reaching, substantive impact on individual Christians, clergy, particular congregations, and denominations. Theologically, the ancient Christian dictum *"Lex orandi, lex credendi "* — meaning "what the Church prays is what it believes" — suggests that if we really want to understand the deepest convictions of a religious body, we should examine its worship.

Although *Prayerfully Pro-Choice* is an anthology with contributions from diverse people, many of the contributions are from RCRC staff, RCRC board members, members of RCRC's Clergy for Choice Network, or persons otherwise formally affiliated with RCRC and its local subdivisions. The resource contains no disclaimer (such as "The views expressed in this notebook do not necessarily represent the position of RCRC"). Rather, the selection and publication of these contributions (sometimes after adaptation by RCRC), from among many submissions, implies that RCRC sanctions these items and endorses the viewpoints espoused in them. Indeed, in a preface to the book, RCRC's President and CEO, Rev. Carlton W. Veazey, refers to the contributions as "spiritually powerful writings" that he hopes will inspire the readers in the "important work" they do.[39] In other words, *Prayerfully Pro-Choice* expresses the theology and spirituality that are the foundation of RCRC's mission.

The primary theological and ethical themes we find in *Prayerfully Pro-Choice* and other RCRC literature are:

- the existence of absolute, God-given sexual and reproductive freedom, including abortion rights;
- the isolation of the woman or teen as sovereign moral agent;
- the trivialization of the moral status of unborn human life;
- the legitimacy of abortion as birth control;
- the holiness of abortion; and

- the sanction of a pro-choice God, attested in Scripture, who blesses all decisions.

These themes are intended to provide the theological and ethical basis for keeping abortion legal and unrestricted.

We will consider each theme in turn. Along the way, we will raise some basic questions about the implications of RCRC's perspectives, though we will not address them until the final section of the book, after we have compared RCRC's position to the positions of its mainline Protestant affiliates.

Boldface italics type has been added to portions of many of the quotations from RCRC literature to highlight the themes; non-boldfaced italicized type is original to the document cited.

The Six Themes

1. Absolute God-given Sexual and Reproductive Freedom, including Abortion Rights

The first key theme in RCRC's literature is the divinely ordained, absolute character of sexual and reproductive freedom, and of the right to abortion.

The following phrase could be RCRC's theological and liturgical mantra: "unfettered freedom." A sample opening litany for "interfaith, pro-choice worship" begins with the leader proclaiming, "Rejoice! For you are called to freedom. You are called to worship and to adore your God, each in your own way and of your own time."[40]

Youth Sexuality

RCRC advocates the wholesomeness of sexual intimacy for teens as well as adults, even apart from marriage. Although this theme is hardly the most prominent in the RCRC literature, it is nonetheless foundational to the entire RCRC project. In 1998, Unitarian Universalist minister Rev. Julie Denny-Hughes, in support of what she called "value-free" sex education, told the Virginia General Assembly that she

> would vehemently oppose any sex education curriculum that instills fear or that presents a single method of preventing pregnancies, namely abstinence. We live in a complex and highly sexualized culture and **our children and young people are naturally curious**. In such an explosive time as this, they need all the defense we can provide to help them **make it through to adulthood without unwanted pregnancy** and without contracting sexually transmitted diseases. (*Prayerfully Pro-Choice*, p. 94)

RCRC's youth organization, Spiritual Youth for Reproductive Freedom (described above), has a vast web site. One of the main goals of this web site is to help young people "[f]ind peace about the choices you've made,"[41] apparently irrespective of the ethical character and consequences of those choices. The choice to carry a child to term, however, is described by RCRC as having to "pay the price."[42] Sexual intimacy is seen as rightful behavior regardless of the consequences, and pregnancy/childbirth as an unfortunate and unnecessary result of a legitimate, moral, spiritual, and honorable youth activity:

> We long for emotional as well as physical closeness; our need is not just to relieve sexual tension but to give and receive love, to bless and be blessed through our touching. So the desire for intercourse can hardly be reduced to its reproductive function.... *Your sexuality is a blessing, not a curse, and your need to express it is to be honored, not despised* — even if that need is the reason you're now facing tough decisions.... *You, and no one else, are "called" to figure out what this unwanted pregnancy is about. And you are to do it without guilt or shame....*[43]

In RCRC's "Breaking the Silence" and "Keeping It Real" sex-education programs, designed primarily for black congregations, church leaders are advised to accept that teenagers and children are inevitably going to be sexually active. The "Keeping It Real" program, for example, is directed at young adolescents who are tired of "moral platitudes and scare tactics about sex."[44] As we will see in Part III, this stance is clearly at odds with the position of most of the Christian churches affiliated with RCRC. They generally teach that sexual activity outside of marriage is inappropriate for Christians and therefore attempt to form their youth for abstinence rather than "safe sex."

The RCRC perspective is also clearly at odds with a recent survey that indicates that youth who are presented with abstinence education in religious settings do in fact delay sexual behavior for positive reasons (faith and morals) rather than out of fear of negative consequences (pregnancy and sexually transmitted diseases).[45]

Abortion Rights

Such a strong emphasis on sexual freedom leads inevitably to a parallel emphasis on abortion rights. Rev. Howard Moody summarizes RCRC's perspective on abortion, not only for women but also for teens. His vision of the future includes "access to the knowledge and means of controlling her reproductive capacity" for every teenager and woman of every marital and socio-economic status and, when contraception fails, access to "a medical facility to **terminate her unwanted and unplanned pregnancy**."[46]

The absolute freedom to choose without restraint is, according to RCRC, the fundamental, divinely granted human, and especially woman's, right. Rev. Moody makes the RCRC point this way:

> My understanding of free choice is that the right to choose is a **God-given right** with which persons are endowed. Without choice, life becomes a meaningless routine and humans become robots. Freedom of choice is what makes us *human* and *responsible*. **And for women, the preeminent freedom is the choice to control her reproductive process**. Any theological or moral arguments that subordinate a woman's freedom to the imaginary screams of a fetus in early pregnancy [a clear reference to the film *The Silent Scream*] or the value of a unique and irreplaceable genetic code in an embryo will be less than human, no matter how much talk there is about "the preciousness of life." (*Prayerfully Pro-Choice*, p. 8)

Similarly, he says, "I would submit that there is **no human right so precious to a woman as the right to choose the time of her childbearing**...."[47]

In a "Ceremony for Closure after an Abortion," Unitarian Universalist minister Rev. Dr. Kendyl Gibbons has the minister say, "Not every essence shall come to be/It is in choosing that we are free."[48] In a similar vein, retired United Methodist Bishop Melvin Talbert interprets Psalm 8 as a text about stewardship and responsibility for something that is not our own, creation, but for which we have responsibility and are "accountable" to God. In the next breath, however, he claims that "God has set us free to be responsible or irresponsible, to be accountable or unaccountable." This self-contradictory theology, which perpetuates the myth of the "sovereign self" (Richard John Neuhaus), is offered as an argument against any political or legal "limiting or taking away our freedom of conscience."[49] The implications of this position, if applied to ecology, geo-politics, or other areas of life and law, are breathtaking.

A related theme in the RCRC literature is the claim that a woman's body is her own sacred possession. Rev. Dr. James Armstrong, a Congregational (United Church of Christ) minister, says that, as the debate over fetal life rages on,

> **the rights of women to control their own bodies are at risk**. A woman's body does not belong to the government. A woman's body does not belong to the church. A woman's body does not

belong to somebody else's conscience. *A woman's body belongs to that woman*. We live in an imperfect world and abortion is always a sad choice. *But a woman has the right to make that choice within the sacred precincts of her own soul*. (*Prayerfully Pro-Choice*, p. 38)

One cannot help but wonder whether Rev. Armstrong has forgotten St. Paul's First Letter to the Corinthians: "[D]o you not know that your body is a temple of the Holy Spirit within you, which you have from God, and that you are not your own? For you were bought with a price; therefore glorify God in your body" (1 Cor. 6:19-20, NRSV).

Justice
RCRC views this unfettered understanding of freedom, and thus of access to unrestricted, affordable abortion, as an essential dimension of social justice, especially for the poor. One of RCRC's chief heroes is the Rev. Dr. Martin Luther King, Jr. RCRC is fond of applying his teachings to the demand for abortion.[50] No mention is made of the irony of interpreting King's commitment to non-violence as justification for support of abortion. (Interestingly, Dr. King drew attention to early Christianity's successful opposition to infanticide in his 1963 *Letter from Birmingham City Jail*.[51]) "To me," writes RCRC President and CEO Rev. Carlton W. Veazey, "the ability to make reproductive choices is *a matter of social justice*, nothing less."[52] (Rev. Veazey is ordained in the National Baptist Convention U.S.A. — with which Dr. King was affiliated until 1961 — and was one of the founders of RCRC's Black Church Initiative.) The theme-text of RCRC's Clergy for Choice Network, announced in its brochure, is Micah 6:8: "...what does the Lord require of you but to do justice...?"

Furthermore, RCRC has constructed a kind of cult of martyrs (in supposed continuity with King and others who died in the struggle for civil rights) by elevating as heroes abortion providers who have been killed for the sake of choice. (Here it must be said emphatically that those who kill abortion providers are not "pro-life," and that the murder of these individuals is abhorrent to us and to God.) A liturgy written by Rev. Roselyn Smith-Withers includes the following lines: "We stand together, remembering the doctors, health care workers and the other innocent people who have *given their lives in the struggle for our right to choose*."[53]

As we will see, RCRC's preoccupation with absolute choice is manifested not only in its view of sex and abortion, but also in its view of God.

2. The Isolation of the Woman or Teen as Sovereign Moral Agent

Closely related to the RCRC notion of the right to choice and to abortion is another theme in the RCRC literature. RCRC contends that abortion is ultimately a woman's (or teenager's) decision made by herself, between herself and her God (however she understands "God").

Isolation

In this decision, the woman or teen alone has absolute, complete freedom and responsibility, although she may consult others. To be sure, RCRC repeatedly affirms that women considering abortion should consult with clergy, doctors, and family (the religious *community* is not mentioned); but in the end, it is the woman alone who has the say and who should be affirmed in her choice, whatever it is. In a booklet and online resource that would appeal especially to teens and young adults, RCRC says, "The decision is yours, but those who are close to you and clearly care about your welfare deserve a chance to be heard."[54]

Contrary to the idea that people of faith have a responsibility to their religious communities, and that they simultaneously benefit from the moral guidance of their tradition and community, RCRC envisions women and teens as untethered moral agents:

> We are religious people who trust women to make wise decisions about whether and when to have children. We affirm women in having children they can welcome, and we affirm women who end pregnancies they feel must not continue.... *We celebrate public policies that acknowledge the moral capacities of individuals....*[55]

Rev. Howard Moody says that "abortion is not a political question" but rather that "the act of having an abortion is the most deeply personal act dealing with a woman's feelings about life, the power of creation and the survival of the species."[56] Similarly, retired United Methodist Bishop Melvin Talbert asserts that there are many people of faith "who believe that choice is the most logical and the most responsible position any religious institution can take on this issue. I feel obliged to make this assertion because choice acknowledges that in the final analysis, *each individual must decide and act.*"[57] This, he avers, is "a matter that is fundamental to our faith... [I]t is the individual who must *search his/her own soul and act on his/her own conscience.*"[58] He continues:

> [T]he time is at hand when we are called to make our declaration of faith. Now is the time for us to stand for the option of choice for women, no matter what. Now is the time for us to remember who

16

women are — ***God's sacred persons who are capable of deciding for themselves what is best.*** (*Prayerfully Pro-Choice*, p. 44)

Similarly, ethicist Paul Simmons, meditating on texts from Genesis 1 and 3, claims, ***"Because the pregnancy is hers, the decision to continue the pregnancy is uniquely hers.*** Like the Creator, she reflects upon what is good for the creation of which she is agent."[59] The parallel Simmons draws between the woman and God is unclear; does he mean to suggest that one way in which God, and by analogy, the woman, can act freely for the good of creation is by destroying part of it? That seems to be the case in Simmons' ecological theology. (One can hardly imagine any remotely similar argument passing muster in a responsible theological discussion of ecology.)

The practical, spiritual consequences of this philosophy are manifested in another piece of RCRC literature entitled *Abortion: Finding Your Own Truth.*[60] In finding her own truth regarding abortion, a pregnant woman is supposed to enter into a meditative position and then:

> ... place both hands over your heart and imagine or remember a time when you were feeling full of love, relaxed, and happy. Notice how your body responds. Where in your body do you experience sensations of warmth, relaxation, softening, and expansiveness? ***This is where your Truth resides.*** Listen to this place as you seek to discover what is right for you.... ***[I]nvite your Loving Spirit to be with you and to guide you.*** Now visualize three doors in front of you.

The three doors represent the choices of birth (and motherhood), abortion, and adoption. The woman is told to imagine each situation, react to it, and then breathe and "release the image" in order to move on. The final piece of counsel is: "Ask yourself: ***Which decision best honors the Truth of who I am?"***

Here the individual is the sovereign arbiter of truth and goodness, acting as her own ethical and religious guide, if not her own deity (notice the capitalized word "Truth"). At no point in this piece of RCRC literature is a pregnant woman urged to make contact with clergy, church or synagogue, Scripture, family, professionals, or anyone other than herself. She is merely to get in touch with her own "Greater Truth, Higher Power, Voice Within, Inner Light, Loving Spirit, Holy Spirit, and Infinite Wisdom." In the same spirit, the concluding song to be used in an abortion decision-making liturgy is "***i found god in myself***" [sic].[61]

17

RCRC tells pregnant women who are considering whether to choose abortion, adoption, or keeping their baby that *"only you can decide which is the right choice for you!*...You may want a baby, but not right now.... You may feel you are too young or too old.... *It's your body. It's your life. It's your choice."*[62] Virginia Ramey Molenkott, in her RCRC article "Respecting the Moral Agency of Women," says, "Only [the pregnant woman] and God can evaluate whether by giving birth at this time she will enhance or destroy the quality of her response to all her other commitments and relationships."[63] At least Molenkott brings God into the picture, but the God she introduces has no explicit relationship to the religious community or tradition in which the woman exists and in which she experiences God.

Teens

Even teens are understood to be such individual moral agents, without any responsibility to — and without the wisdom of — their parents. RCRC suggests that the abortion decision need not involve parents, even in the case of minors. In *Barriers to Abortion are Barriers to Justice for Women*, RCRC states, "Laws that require physicians to notify or gain consent of parents — or that require teens to go to court to obtain a judge's permission — serve no useful purpose."[64] At the end of this article, RCRC expresses the view that "many women feel that abortion is not so much a choice as a necessity."[65] But RCRC does not seem to realize that if a parent and a religious community were involved in a teenager's choice, she might not see abortion as such an urgent "necessity."

A 21-year-old woman who opted for abortion when she was 16 is quoted approvingly by RCRC:

> I knew I was pregnant from the very moment — and I knew from the core of my being that it was wrong. Even though I love children, I had no doubt that an abortion would be the right thing in this particular situation. That was five years ago, and every time I think about it I always have the same feeling — relief, almost a sense of deliverance. It would have been unbearable to have had to live with that mistake for a lifetime. My life was changed in this experience, transformed. I like to think I'm stronger now, more able to be my own person. I can't help think that making that decision was probably the beginning of a new life for me. It was probably when *I became an adult....* (*Prayerfully Pro-Choice*, p. 25)

For RCRC, then, abortion is not only a *right*; it may also be a *rite* — a rite of passage to adulthood. To make a life-changing choice for abortion in isolation seems to be the quintessential act of womanhood.

3. The Trivialization of the Moral Status of Unborn Human Life
So far we have focused solely on the rights of teens and women, according to RCRC. We turn now to what RCRC says about life *in utero*. RCRC literature sends a mixed and even self-contradictory message about the status of the human embryo and fetus. Despite presenting an official line of respect for "potential" human life, RCRC literature both implicitly and explicitly reveals a different position.

Yes and No
Officially, RCRC "honor[s] the value and dignity of all human life" and "recognize[s] that different religious traditions hold a variety of views regarding when life begins." Therefore, it says, "because of these honest differences, and because we live in a society where all are free to live according to their own consciences and religious beliefs," RCRC "believe[s] no one religious philosophy should govern the law for all Americans."[66] It also claims to "hold in high respect the value of potential human life, while remaining committed to women as responsible, moral decision-makers."[67]

This official respect emerges in some worship resources, but always with a major exception clause — the overriding principle of the woman's right to choose. For example, an interfaith liturgy for choice has a prayer litany that includes the words, "We pray for women who *know that life is beginning within them*, who face the agony of wondering what to do about it when they cannot cope."[68] This is to be followed by the response, "Give us the strength to meet what we must face." It also has a prayer for "doctors and nurses who daily *hold the powers of life and death in their hands*," which is supposed to be concluded with the words, "Enable our *compassionate caring for human life at every stage*."

These contradictions — prayers affirming unborn human life in the context of "pro-choice worship" — can only be explained by another part of the opening litany, in which all present are supposed to say, "We rejoice in the freedom to love and to sanctify life — though we cherish all life, *we would not diminish its quality in others*." The absolute moral principle is freedom, and human life (other than my own) be damned, if necessary. Once again, even the thought of applying such a moral principle to other spheres of human existence is chilling.

This self-contradictory ethic appears also in another prayer litany, this one as part of a service for those who have died in the pro-choice cause:

> Leader: We pray for **freedom to choose** — to choose to have children, but also **to choose not to have children**.
>
> All: Enable our **compassionate caring for human life at every stage and in every form**. (*Prayerfully Pro-Choice*, p. 74)

It is difficult to resist the logical conclusion that for RCRC sometimes "compassionate caring for human life at every stage and in every form" includes the termination of that life.

Fetal Non-personhood
The elevation of choice to an absolute value can lead to a more explicit rejection of the value of unborn human life. Despite its formal acknowledgment of a diversity of religious views on the status of the fetus, RCRC reveals its own position, articulated by Rev. Howard Moody, with stunning epistemological certainty: "**While we are certain that it is not a human being**, equal in any way to the life of the mother, it is a form of 'potential life.'"[69]

Thus, following the claims of Moody and others, Paul Simmons constructs for RCRC a biblical argument to deny the proposition that the fetus is, in any sense, a "person" with rights, or that a "potential person" might have rights. (To put the issue the other way around, RCRC does not believe that the already-born have any obligations to the not-yet-born.)

This is a very complex issue, but it surely demands more intellectual rigor than the kind of ideologically driven, simplistic biblical literalism that Simmons practices. In *Prayerfully Pro-Choice* and in several articles,[70] Simmons argues from the opening chapters of Genesis that to be a "person" requires breathing (Gen. 2:7); possessing godlike spiritual, personal, relational, moral, and intellectual capabilities; and choice-making (Gen. 3:22):

> The biblical portrait of person, therefore, is that of a complex, many-sided creature with godlike abilities and the moral responsibility to make choices. **The fetus hardly meets those characteristics**.... The abortion question focuses on the personhood of the woman, who in turn considers the potential personhood of

the fetus in terms of the multiple dimensions of her own history and future. (*Prayerfully Pro-Choice*, p. 117[71])

Once again, we ought to find the implications of such claims chilling. If this represents a Christian understanding of personhood, who else is excluded? How else can one manipulate a biblical text about the creation of healthy, adult humans to define non-personhood? Yet for RCRC, the non-humanity or non-personhood of the embryo and fetus has become one of its fundamental doctrines: "*Legally, a human being is one who is born. Biblically, it is one who breathes.*"[72]

A still more radical trivialization of unborn human life can be found in comments from Rev. Howard Moody. After painting a caricature of the right-to-life position and suggesting that an embryo or fetus has no divine rights, Moody lambasts abortion opponents, calling their position "idolatry" and making his own views explicit:

> For those who know their religious history, the deification of the *conceptus* is as heretical an idolatry as any pagan practice whereby a human was sacrificed for the sake of some idolized animal, stone, or tree.... On the basis of this *spurious heresy of the deification of the fetus*, they ["religious anti-choice people"] consign a woman to bear and care for *the result of conception* so that body, mind, and spirit are bound by a biological determination and prevent her from ever knowing true liberty.... Birth ought never to be forced, compelled or mandated by another person or the state itself. *Rights begin with birth* — they are a birthday present — *birthright*. (*Prayerfully Pro-Choice*, p. 8)

The logical, semantic, theological, and historical confusion exhibited in this quotation deserves a rebuttal that space, unfortunately, does not permit. Aside from that issue, however, the text reveals an evaluation of the fetus as possessing no moral or legal rights until birth. Moody does not even allow for the existence of fetal rights or fetal intrinsic value by virtue of human life being a gift from God, even though he himself affirms birth as a divine gift.

A Lutheran (ELCA) pastor who serves on RCRC's Clergy Advisory Board, Rev. Dr. Charles V. Bergstrom, summarizes RCRC's self-contradictory theology and impoverished understanding of personhood: "Lutherans believe that life is a gift from God. That life begins at the time of conception in some form.... However, a fetus is not a person. As the 14th Amendment [of the U.S. Constitution] says, we are born or naturalized as citizens...."[73] This curious blending of theological authorities — the

Christian theological tradition and the U.S. Constitution — accounts in large measure for the self-contradictory character of RCRC's theological reasoning.

With such a low estimation of unborn human life (which many Lutherans and other Christians reject), RCRC does *not* contradict itself on one matter: affirming the legitimacy of abortion as birth control, as we will now see.

4. The Legitimacy of Abortion as Birth Control

People of good will disagree about what circumstances and motives make an abortion a form of birth control. Part of the problem may be in defining the term "birth control." Fundamentally, it refers to methods of preventing childbirth without refraining from sex. Birth control can take two basic forms, pregnancy prevention and pregnancy termination. In the latter case, abortion as birth control implies broadly that the abortion is sought, not because the pregnancy is medically dangerous to the woman or fetus, but because the pregnancy is not desired. (This, as RCRC rightly stresses, does not mean that such an abortion is "convenient.")

RCRC's own literature, based on the work of the Alan Guttmacher Institute, reports that nearly half of all pregnancies are unintended, and that half of those end in abortion. Two-thirds of women who abort have never been married; black women are three times more likely than white women to seek an abortion. The Guttmacher Institute notes that women who seek abortion do so primarily for the following kinds of reasons:

- 75% say that having a baby would interfere with work, school, or other responsibilities;
- 67% say that the cost of a child is too high; and
- 50% say that they do not want to be a single parent or are having relationship problems with the partner/husband.[74]

The Guttmacher Institute has found that almost one million teens become pregnant annually. For 78% of these teens, the pregnancy is unplanned, and about 35% of those who do not miscarry will get an abortion. The main reasons for teen abortion are concerns about how a baby would affect their lives, feelings of immaturity, and fear of finances.[75]

The Guttmacher Institute and RCRC also say that 54% of the women who obtain abortions became pregnant while using birth control. This suggests that many of those women use abortion as their secondary or substitute form of birth control when contraception fails.[76] This statistic also suggests that many of the other 46% seek abortions as their primary means of birth control because they had not used contraception. The

Institute also reports that 13% of abortions are chosen in part because of a possible fetal defect, and 7% out of concern for the woman's own health.[77]

Given these statistics, including those that indicate the relative rarity of medically dangerous pregnancies in the United States, it is difficult to resist the conclusion that abortion is frequently used as a means of birth control. However, whether the percentage of birth-control abortions is 25%, 50%, or more, RCRC presents abortion as a moral and even *holy* means of dealing with *any* pregnancy, including pregnancy when contraception has failed and the pregnancy is unwanted. That effectively makes the claim that abortion is a legitimate form of birth control. This perspective pervades RCRC literature. (We will document and explain the claim of "holiness" in point 5 below.)

Choice as a Religious Experience
RCRC makes the abortion-as-birth-control decision a religious experience: "Your pregnancy — any pregnancy — is a call to discover God's intentions...," a call to which the woman may say "yes" or "no."[78] A woman contemplating abortion should offer a prayer (which originated on an anniversary of *Roe v. Wade*) to the creator who grants "courage and intelligence to make decisions about our childbearing," for "we are required to attend with care to our health and well-being."[79] As noted above, Rev. Howard Moody's emphasis on absolute choice means his vision of a day when every woman, at any time, has access to "a medical facility to terminate her **unwanted and unplanned** pregnancy."[80] This perspective is summarized more bluntly by Whoopi Goldberg and quoted in *Prayerfully Pro-Choice*: "***The bottom line is that if someone does not want to have a child they [sic] should not be forced into it.***"[81]

Thus a prayer in the memorial service for those who have died in the pro-choice cause reads:

> Help us, Gracious God... to rededicate ourselves to continue the work of securing and maintaining all reproductive health care options for all people.... *We pray for freedom to choose — to choose to have children, but also to choose not to have children....* Give us strengthened dedication as we seek reproductive freedom.... Let us never be satisfied until each person and each group is extended reproductive freedom. (*Prayerfully Pro-Choice*, pp. 73-74)

This is nothing other than a prayer for legally and divinely sanctioned access to abortion as a form of birth control.

An even more forceful word on this subject is a benediction written by feminist liturgist and psychotherapist Diann L. Neu, in her "Litany of Challenge." Her benediction encourages pro-choice worshipers to go forth to "the city centers and the country corners to tell women that *all of their choices, including their choice for abortion, are holy and healthy.*"[82] This, we might say, is the RCRC equivalent of the Great Commission in Matthew 28, for RCRC exhorts the faithful to preach the gospel of holy and healthy choice, of holy and healthy abortion. The same litany also urges them to "encourage rabbis, ministers, priests and counselors to counsel women on free choice."

Diann Neu also provides a liturgy to assist a woman who "discovers she is *unintentionally pregnant*" by helping her "focus on *whether to bring her pregnancy to term or to have an abortion.*"[83] In the liturgy, participants invoke "Gracious and loving Holy Wisdom" so that the woman may "know clearly the choice that she needs to make"; they then petition Holy Wisdom to "[b]less her and comfort her with your Spirit." Another liturgy from Diann Neu, called "Affirming a Choice," is prefaced by an assertion that women's friends, ministers, and counselors "need to develop and celebrate *liturgies that affirm women's reproductive choices*." A prayer to "Mother Goddess and Father God" includes praise "that you have given your people the power of choice," bemoans the circumstances that were "such that she has had to choose to terminate her pregnancy," and "*rejoice[s] in her attention to choice.*"[84]

RCRC's Eschatological Vision
RCRC's conviction about abortion as a legitimate form of birth control is not merely applied to individuals, but is part of a global vision once again couched in religious language. A 1999 speech by Marjorie Signer of RCRC and Cynthia Cooper of the Center for Reproductive Law and Policy, on the Day of Six Billion (October 12, 1999 — the day the population of the earth is supposed to have reached 6,000,000,000) proclaims the following:

> The proper stewardship of human reproduction should result in a blessing for the peoples of the world and for the Earth in general. For this reason, we must strive to ensure that the birth of each child is a blessing for that child, for his or her family, and for the world in general. We must strive to ensure that families have reproductive choices that they may freely make... [including] safe, legal, and affordable abortion services for women who make that choice.... (*Prayerfully Pro-Choice*, p. 98)

The writers place this argument for abortion as birth control in the context of stewardship and social justice, contending that affordable abortion is a requirement for the fulfillment of Isaiah's eschatological vision of a new heaven and a new earth (Isa. 65:17-25). In this vision, infant mortality and other threats to children do not exist, and there is no enmity, violence, or destruction. In RCRC's interpretation of Isaiah's vision, however, children should be allowed to be born if and only if they somehow meet some arbitrary criterion (established by whom?) of being a "blessing." We should not permit the religious language to mask the radical perspective expressed here: human life is being judged not as inherently valuable but only as a means to an end. When it does not meet that subjective end, it may be destroyed — *in the name of God*. The extrapolation of this thesis is somber.

Clergy Support

RCRC's commitment to abortion as birth control is heard also in the individual statements of clergy, which are provided as resources for worship. Some of these statements are from clergy whose denominations officially oppose their view of abortion as an acceptable form of birth control.

Individual statements in *Prayerfully Pro-Choice* include the remarks of a Unitarian Universalist minister:

> [W]e believe that the test of any religious position is an individual's own direct experience of the good, the holy and the true. Because of that starting point, Unitarian Universalism supports a woman's right of choice in reproductive matters, including the **right to choose to terminate an unwanted pregnancy**. (*Prayerfully Pro-Choice*, p. 103)

A Presbyterian (PCUSA) minister, Rev. Kenneth Applegate, makes the same point with a slightly more Christian vocabulary:

> If a woman is pregnant, we recognize and affirm how difficult it is to **decide whether to continue with the pregnancy or not**. We will **support her and her partner in whatever choice is made** as they are guided by Scripture and the Holy Spirit.... Presbyterians believe that...we have a responsibility to determine when and how we will be partners with God in creating new life. (*Prayerfully Pro-Choice*, p. 110)

Thus, when RCRC's pamphlet inviting clergy to join the Clergy for Choice Network includes the Network's "pledge" — "We... pledge our strong support for reproductive choice [including]... access to safe, legal and affordable abortion" — we know with assurance that this means abortion as birth control, abortion for unwanted pregnancies, abortion as the exercise of free choice. Or, more directly, as one RCRC article puts it: *"If... you feel that you have no responsibility to preserve a new life until it becomes personlike [however you define that], your moral freedom to end it exists up to that point."*[85]

5. *The Holiness of Abortion*

In looking at RCRC texts about abortion as birth control, we have also seen that RCRC materials sometimes describe the abortion decision as a holy act. We now need to focus specifically on this claim of sanctity, for perhaps the most radical theme in the RCRC literature is its contention that the promotion of abortion rights, the provision of abortion services, the thoughtful decision to abort, and the abortion itself are all divinely sanctioned and "holy" activities. To be sure, abortion is seen as an unfortunate and painful circumstance. Nevertheless, with striking self-confidence and relentless conviction, in *Prayerfully Pro-Choice* RCRC depicts abortion as a sacred act.

"Holy Choices"

As we noted above, in a "Litany of Challenge," worshipers leave to proclaim the gospel of abortion as a *"holy"* choice.[86] In a "Ceremony for Closure after an Abortion," Unitarian Universalist minister Rev. Dr. Kendyl Gibbons has the minister affirm first the holiness of every night a child is born, and then also the abortion decision: "The choice that _____ and _____ have made is also a *sacred choice*; a choice for coherence and responsibility in life."[87]

Those, therefore, who advocate for abortion rights are performing a holy task. As we saw above, retired United Methodist Bishop Talbert proclaims that people of faith stand for choice because "we believe *God calls us to this hour*."[88]

Also holy is the work of those who assist women in exercising their free choice. A "Service of Memory and Dedication" includes a prayer "for all those persons, both lay and clergy, who *do your holy work* of listening to and helping women sort out their options," asking the "Source of Wisdom, Spirit of Love" to "[g]ive them a portion of your gentle and nurturing spirit so that their guidance will uphold and respect each woman's own conscience and beliefs."[89] The liturgy called "Affirming a Choice," by Diann Neu, is prefaced by an assertion that women's friends, ministers, and counselors "need to develop and celebrate liturgies that affirm women's reproductive choices"; thus this liturgy "affirms that a woman *has made a good and holy decision to have an abortion*."[90]

"Holy Work"

It follows also, then, that abortion providers perform holy work. In a 1997 sermon to the National Abortion Federation (doctors, administrators, counselors, and activists in abortion provision), Episcopal priest and former RCRC Board Chair Rev. Dr. Katherine Hancock Ragsdale concluded with a comparison of the "difficult" and "dangerous" work of abortion providers to that of civil-rights leaders. She then compared the situation to that of the prophets recalled by Jesus in the Beatitudes (Matt. 5:11-12: "Blessed are you when people revile you and persecute you... falsely... on my account, for in the same way they persecuted the prophets who were before you"), leading to a benediction that went as follows: "May She bless us all and grant each of us a full measure of faith and courage as we commit ourselves to this *sacred work*."[91]

RCRC encourages its affiliates to develop "religious convocation[s] at the local level" to bear "faithful witness for choice."[92] Instead of holding a press conference to announce such a convocation, an "alternative 'visibility event'" might be to gather "[m]embers of the clergy (and political leaders) appearing in front of a clinic [that provides abortion services] *to 'bless' the work they do*... [as] a powerful symbol of support for reproductive choice."[93]

In 1998, Rev. Cynthia S. Bumb, a United Church of Christ minister and executive director of the Missouri RCRC, offered a "blessing" at a new Planned Parenthood facility, expressing "gratitude" for Planned Parenthood's work, for its work "is *holy work, service provided by God's people on behalf of God's people*." She also prayed for "*God's gracious blessing upon this work*, upon this facility and upon all those who will pass through these doors." The blessing concluded, "May Planned Parenthood continue to be an *instrument of your service*, doing the *holy work of healing and caring for your creation*. O Holy One, may it be so. And let the people say, Amen!"[94] Similarly, Rev. David Selzer, an Episcopal priest who is the director of Concerned Clergy for Choice and the convener of the Western New York RCRC, offers a blessing to be used for "providers of women's health care":

> Gracious Provider of Care and Protection/*Bless this building and those who work here*/The doctors and nurses and other health care workers/Who provide safe, legal, caring and loving reproductive services, including abortion, to women in need/Who recognize the rights of women to make reproductive choices/*They are doing*

God's work/We celebrate their concern and commitment." (*Prayerfully Pro-Choice*, p. 101)

In summary, then, we may say: For RCRC, abortion is God's work. It is holy.

6. A Pro-Choice God, Attested in Scripture, Who Blesses All Decisions

According to RCRC, abortion is "God's work." Furthermore, the RCRC god is a "pro-choice" deity whose primary role in human affairs is to assist people in finding and following their own truth. This deity is therefore a god who offers unquestioned sustenance and support in a woman's pursuit of the best choice for her, according to her.

Divine Presence and Blessing

One of the prominent themes in RCRC liturgical resources is the presence of God in times of difficult decisions; few religious people would dispute this claim. But many RCRC liturgies often baldly state, and others imply, that God's presence is equivalent to God's approval. A prayer from an interfaith service contains these words: "We accept the responsibility, claim the tradition and we embrace **the right to choose prayerfully with the knowledge that God is with us** in all of our circumstances."[95]

This deity is a "hands-off" god who, RCRC avers in celebration of *Roe v. Wade*, has blessed women with "courage and intelligence to make decisions about our childbearing."[96] In contrast to the biblical image of humans waiting for God, one RCRC prayer repeatedly addresses God with the words, "You wait for us!" The same prayer asserts that "[a]lways we are guided by your sovereign power.... Always we are accepted by your unconditional love."[97]

In her liturgy "Affirming a Choice," Diann Neu includes an unqualified human affirmation of any woman who has chosen abortion as a mirror of the divine attitude: "We affirm her and support her in her decision. We promise to stand with her in her ongoing life. **Blessed are you, Holy Wisdom, for your presence with her.**"[98]

Rev. Julia Mayo Quinlan, ordained in both The United Methodist Church and the American Baptist Churches, claims in a sermon to resonate with the theological viewpoint of Whoopi Goldberg, whose book *The Choices We Made* Rev. Quinlan quotes:

> "I talk about God because God and I are very close. God gives you choice. God gives you freedom of choice. That's in the Bible. I have this deep belief that God understands whatever dilemma you're in and will forgive it. You make a choice that He or She

doesn't think is right — that's God's prerogative." (*Prayerfully Pro-Choice*, p. 35)

This deity is all-forgiving, without qualification or repentance; Ms. Goldberg and Rev. Quinlan do not introduce the concept of "repentance" into their theology of forgiveness, but at least there is a hint of possible divine displeasure at certain choices for abortion (a hint that is absent from nearly every piece of RCRC literature). However, immediately after quoting Whoopi Goldberg, Rev. Quinlan ends her sermon by encouraging her listeners to "discern the movement of God's Spirit in freedom and choice."[99] This is closer to the RCRC party line than Whoopi Goldberg's near-allusion to human sin. In other circumstances, such sweeping theological claims have been referred to as "cheap grace" (Dietrich Bonhoeffer). The only question here is which version of grace is cheaper: the grace offered by Whoopi Goldberg's deity, who at least has the "prerogative" to disapprove, or the grace offered by RCRC's deity.

In a similar "Ceremony for Closure after an Abortion," Unitarian Universalist minister Rev. Dr. Kendyl Gibbons affirms choice without qualification and suggests that her rather pan-entheistic deity also relieves all feelings of guilt, grief, and loss. She writes:

> We have gathered today to honor the importance of a decision.... We give them [an unmarried man and woman in a "committed relationship"] our support in the act by which they would release the energy and creativity which might have been their child, from the bonds of their grief and guilt, into the fathomless universe of potential, there to find other form.... With loving grief, we release that potential to other incarnations in the infinite womb of the universe, from which nothing is ever lost. (*Prayerfully Pro-Choice*, pp. 85-86)

One of the most explicit affirmations of God's approval of choice comes in the pamphlet *Considering Abortion? Clarifying What You Believe*. In it, RCRC says, "You are to claim your godlike, God-given role in creation by saying yes or no, secure in the knowledge that *whatever you decide, after having honestly sought what is right, God will bless*."[100]

The Deity "Choice"

RCRC has so elevated "choice" that it has become the highest value and virtue in the organization's symbolic world. Such homage is paid to choice, in fact, that we might do well to write the word with an initial capital letter — "Choice" — because it has become personified and even deified in that symbolic world. Like ancient Greece and Rome, which formed gods such as Fortune and Justice out of cultural values, RCRC and the culture of choice have created a divinity out of their highest value. It is called Choice.

In this theology and worldview, there are absolutely no criteria to guide or evaluate decisions. The god or goddess Choice, which makes no demands on its worshipers — other than to pursue what is right for oneself and, especially, to choose freely — has been honored.

This is *not* to say that RCRC has no ethic; it does. Many RCRC writers envision a world of justice for children, women, and the entire human family. They certainly have a sense that there is good and evil in the world, and that God wills goodness. The abortion decision is envisioned as a means to achieving a greater degree of the divine goodness in the world. However, RCRC's prior commitment to abortion rights (and thus choice) has affected its understanding of God and caused RCRC to re-fashion God in the image of the pro-choice movement. As in other RCRC themes we have examined, the notion that God is first and foremost the promoter of choice, even choice for the (supposed) good of the world, is a chilling and potentially dangerous theology.

Conclusion: Abortion as Holy War

In the many quotations from RCRC literature that we have examined, we have seen six closely interrelated themes emerge. These can be summarized as follows:

> *Abortion is a divinely blessed and guided act that can be practiced by a sovereign, isolated moral agent without regard to any external moral or legal restraints and without concern about the moral status of the target of the act.*

Those who are even somewhat familiar with theories about ethics — or with contemporary political discussions — will hear in this summary echoes of the tradition of holy war. In fact, RCRC's position on abortion can best be understood by analogy to the ethical issue of war in the Christian tradition.

There have been three basic Christian positions on war over the centuries: pacifism, or non-participation in war; the just-war tradition; and the holy-war or crusade tradition. These positions emerged in this order chronologically. In contemporary mainstream Christian ethics, only two of these positions (with many variations) remain formally intact: pacifism and just-war theory. The holy-war tradition has been dismissed as inappropriate, and as essentially both idolatrous and heretical for Christians.

In the just-war tradition, lethal violence is justified only as a last resort and with many strict moral and ethical guidelines. War is acknowledged as something not to celebrate, but to avoid at almost all costs. Theoretically, war should be prosecuted humbly and penitently. Enemies are to be treated as human beings, and non-combatants are not to be targeted. The idea of God willing or blessing war is rejected. In a world of evils, war may occasionally be morally justified in human terms, *but it is not holy.*

In the holy-war tradition, war is understood as a divine vocation that is therefore blessed and guided by God. Anyone (head of state, terrorist, etc.) who proposes or prosecutes such a war is not accountable to any legal or moral principles, but only to his or her own sense of divine calling and approval. Because the war is sanctioned by God, no one can question its moral or legal legitimacy, and no one can determine the conditions under which it is appropriate or the means by which it may be waged. Innocent persons (e.g., non-combatants) may be targeted without culpability. The whole enterprise of war is seen as a right and even as a religious duty.[101]

The holy-war or crusade mentality has not been completely purged from the spirituality of the Christian Church or from American civil religion. At times, it must be admitted, this mentality has infected organizations and individuals who wear a "pro-life" badge but whose actions are hardly pro-life or Christian. Sadly, it has even led to lethal violence. For this, there is no excuse.

For very good reasons, no contemporary Christian theologian, mainline church, or legitimate Christian organization espouses the dangerous and uncontrollable holy-war tradition with respect to war. *Nevertheless, RCRC's perspective on abortion is analogous to the holy-war tradition. The six RCRC themes that we have considered reproduce fundamental features of the holy-war tradition:*

- the absence of external moral or legal restraints;
- the isolation and sovereignty of the moral agent;
- the lack of concern for the moral status of the targets;
- the absence of criteria to justify the action;
- the holiness of the act; and
- the blessing of God.

The presence of anything like a holy-war mentality in a religious organization ought to raise grave concerns among its members. In the case of RCRC and the Christian churches affiliated with it in any way, the concerns of the churches should be very serious, since these churches have by and large maintained a "just-war," or last-resort, approach to abortion, as we will now see.

III. Considering the Statements of RCRC Member Bodies

IN LIGHT OF RCRC'S LITERATURE and evident positive stance toward abortion as an acceptable, divinely sanctioned form of birth control, as well as its focus on "finding your own truth," a consideration of member groups' position statements on these issues is now in order. Given the limitations of this small book, a comprehensive look at the positions of all member organizations is not possible. Rather, the following overview confines itself to the major Christian denominations that are represented among RCRC's member groups. Their views should not be taken to be representative of all member groups. In fact, in various dimensions of this issue, no conclusive agreement exists among all members, and RCRC openly admits that members maintain widely differing perspectives as to when abortion is morally justified.

Nonetheless, when RCRC issues statements or approaches elected representatives, it presumes to speak for mainline Protestant Christians. To be just in its activities, it should honestly represent all member organizations' views. It should attempt to clarify, both to the public and to legislators, that certain members, despite their support for legal abortion, hold very serious reservations regarding abortion. As the following discussion will show, in light of the previous analysis of RCRC's position, RCRC's "holy-war" approach to abortion fails to represent the grave reservations that its own Christian members have about abortion.

Currently there are four mainline Protestant denominations with units that are members of RCRC: The United Methodist Church, the Presbyterian Church (USA), the Episcopal Church in the USA, and the United Church of Christ. In general, it is these bodies' divisions of women's concerns and/or social justice that are affiliated with RCRC. (For specifics, see Appendix A.)

Like RCRC, these denominations officially share a general commitment to keeping abortion legal.[102] But as we read the *theological* statements of these mainline churches, we find a number of basic common themes. Despite some superficial similarities to the perspective of RCRC, these themes are fundamentally at odds with those we found in the RCRC documents.

In sum, RCRC treats abortion as a holy, moral, liberating, empowering, divine gift and right. Three of the four affiliated mainline Protestant churches — and even to some degree the fourth member (the United Church of Christ) — view abortion as a tragic last resort that should generally be avoided and cannot be easily condoned. *This is a fundamental and indeed antithetical difference between the RCRC and the mainline Protestant churches.* The difference is parallel to the radical difference between those who espouse a "holy-war" or crusade mentality and those who are part of the just-war tradition and regretfully admit the occasional necessity of lethal violence as a last resort. As noted above, the Christian churches long ago saw the error of the holy-war mentality and have done their best to distance themselves from that perspective. The same distancing from RCRC's "holy-abortion" mentality must now take place.

Four basic theological and ethical themes about abortion that we find in the official positions of these mainline churches are:

- responsible, covenantal sex within marriage;
- decision making in Christian community;
- the sacredness of unborn human life; and
- abortion only as a reluctantly sanctioned last resort and not as a means of birth control.

Similar themes may be found in the statements of churches that have left RCRC or never affiliated with it, including the Moravian Church, the American Baptist Churches, and the Evangelical Lutheran Church in America, each of which we shall also briefly consider.

The discovery of "just-war theory" in discussions of abortion is no accident. It reveals the way in which mainline Protestant churches have attempted to find a moderating theological and ethical position on the abortion issue. In fact, in 1987 *The Christian Century* — a very influential periodical in the mainline Protestant churches — published an article by Unitarian minister F. Forrester Church called "A Just-War Theory for Abortion."[103] In 1991, United Church of Christ theologian Gabriel Fackre and his wife, Dorothy Ashman Fackre, contributed a careful "just abortion" article to the *Handbook of Themes for Preaching*.[104] The spirit, if not the exact content, of those articles permeates the statements we are about to examine.[105]

In the following quotations, key phrases have been placed in boldface italics.

The United Methodist Church

The most recent comprehensive church statement on abortion by a denomination affiliated with RCRC is the 2000 statement of The United Methodist Church (UMC), which may amend the "Social Principles" in its *Book of Discipline* every four years at the church's General Conference. The United Methodist Church has been involved with RCAR/RCRC since the group's founding. (Technically, not the church, but two of its divisions — the General Board of Church and Society and the General Board of

Global Ministries, Women's Division — hold membership in RCRC.) In 1992, General Convention delegates narrowly rejected (485-448) a resolution to withdraw from RCAR, but a few months later the church's Judicial Council issued a decision that its boards' membership in RCAR was consistent with the church's "Social Principles."[106] In the same year, the Methodists adopted a reaffirmation of *Roe v. Wade.*[107] The web site of the church's General Board of Church and Society has an article about, and a link to, RCRC's youth initiative.[108]

The church's position on abortion as a moral and theological concern has evolved, though its 2000 version differs from the 1996 text only by the addition of a sentence about partial-birth abortion.[109] As of 2000, the church's official position, preserved in the "Social Principles," says:

> The beginning of life and the ending of life are the God-given boundaries of human existence. While individuals have always had some degree of control over when they would die, they now have the awesome power to determine when and even whether new individuals will be born. Our belief in the *sanctity of unborn human life* makes us *reluctant to approve abortion*. But we are equally bound to respect the sacredness of the life and well-being of the mother, for whom devastating damage may result from an unacceptable pregnancy. In continuity with past Christian teaching, we recognize tragic *conflicts of life with life that may justify abortion*, and in such cases we support the legal option of abortion under proper medical procedures. *We cannot affirm abortion as an acceptable means of birth control, and we unconditionally reject it as a means of gender selection.*[110] We oppose the use of late-term abortion known as dilation and extraction (partial-birth abortion) and call for the end of this practice except when the physical life of the mother is in danger and no other medical procedure is available, or in the case of severe fetal anomalies incompatible with life.

The statement continues:

> We call all Christians to a searching and prayerful *inquiry into the sorts of conditions that may warrant abortion*. We commit our Church to continue to provide nurturing ministries to those who terminate a pregnancy, to those in the midst of a crisis pregnancy, and to those who give birth.[111] Governmental laws and regulations do not provide all the guidance required by the informed Christian

conscience. Therefore, a decision concerning abortion should be made only after thoughtful and prayerful consideration by the parties involved, *with medical, pastoral, and other appropriate counsel.*[112]

The United Methodist Church, then, in contrast to RCRC, affirms its reluctance to approve abortion, its belief in "the sanctity of unborn human life," and the necessity of assistance in decision making. It explicitly rejects abortion as birth control and places restrictions on its being considered at all ("tragic conflicts of life with life"). Partial-birth abortion is permitted only in extreme cases.

Although The United Methodist Church's statement does not explicitly use the words "last resort," it echoes this aspect of the just-war tradition in several ways. The statement uses the language of reluctance, speaks of "tragic conflicts," mentions "conditions that may warrant abortion," and at various points offers actual criteria for unacceptable and possibly acceptable abortion. Also, the phrase "In continuity with past Christian tradition" suggests an analogy to the just-war tradition (which The United Methodist Church also accepts only with serious hesitation[113]) and suggests a cautious, tradition-guided approach to abortion that differs significantly from the typical American (and RCRC) approach that focuses on individual rights. Moreover, the church states that the quest for what conditions might (and therefore might not) justify abortion is not over, and that government regulations are insufficient to satisfy that quest. Finally, the denominations's rejection of partial-birth abortion not only differs from RCRC's position; it also reveals the influence of a philosophy of last-resort: only under certain extreme conditions is it permitted.

Furthermore, on the subject of sex, the *Discipline* says that "[a]lthough all persons are sexual beings whether or not they are married, sexual relations are only clearly affirmed in the marriage bond."[114] This, too, is in stark contrast to RCRC's position.

In sum, then, The United Methodist Church rejects RCRC's approval of unfettered sexual relations and abortion as birth control; it sanctifies what RCRC trivializes (unborn human life); and it insists on the Christian tradition as the context for decision making. Although this position hardly rules out all abortions, it clearly does not reflect RCRC's theology or ethics.

The Presbyterian Church (USA)

The Presbyterian Church (USA), or PC(USA), maintains ties to RCRC through various offices of its National Ministries Division, including the

Office of Women's Ministries and a body called Presbyterians Affirming Reproductive Options, which is a constituency group of the Presbyterian Health, Education and Welfare Association and is affiliated with the church's National Ministries Division.[115] Like The United Methodist Church and unlike RCRC, the Presbyterian Church (USA) does not approve of sexual activity outside of marriage, advocates the protection of all life, and has strong reservations about abortion.

In 1992, at the 204th General Assembly, the PC(USA) issued its most recent general position statement on abortion. Excerpts from that statement follow in this block quote and in subsequent paragraphs:

> We affirm the ability and responsibility of women, guided by the Scriptures and the Holy Spirit, *in the context of their communities of faith*, to make good moral choices in regard to problem pregnancies.... We are *disturbed by abortions that seem to be elected only as a convenience or to ease embarrassment*. We affirm that abortion should *not be used as a method of birth control*. Abortion is not morally acceptable for gender selection only.... The strong Christian presumption is that since *all life is precious to God*, we are to preserve and protect it. Abortion ought to be an option of *last resort*. The large number of abortions in this society is a grave concern to the church.... While Presbyterians do not have substantial agreement on when human life begins, we do have agreement that taking human life is sin. By affirming the ability and responsibility of a woman to make good moral choices, *the Presbyterian Church (USA) does not advocate abortion* but instead acknowledges circumstances in a sinful world that may make abortion the least objectionable of difficult options.[116]

Like The United Methodist Church, the Presbyterian Church (USA) differs markedly from the RCRC even though it echoes RCRC's conviction that women are competent moral agents and affirms abortion as a legal option. (It says early in the document that "no law should deny access to safe and affordable [abortion] services.") In harmony with the Methodists, Presbyterians affirm decision making "in the context of their [women's] communities of faith"; reject abortion as birth control, for convenience, and for gender selection; affirm that "all life [in context meaning especially life *in utero*] is precious to God"; and express reluctance to approve abortion, calling it explicitly an "option of last resort."

Moreover, the 1992 statement also claims that there are criteria for a "morally acceptable" abortion, among which are indications of severe fetal deformity, rape or incest, or endangerment to the "physical or mental health of either woman or child." The document does not, however, unequivocally say that the embryo/fetus is [inviolable] "human life," for "Presbyterians hold varying points of view about when human life begins."

The Presbyterians' appeal to the language of "last resort" and to Christianity's "strong presumption" to "preserve and protect" all human life stems from the general Christian moral tradition of presumption against killing and its specific manifestation in the just-war tradition. That also explains their appeal to criteria for a justifiable abortion, even if some of the criteria (e.g. "mental health") can be interpreted quite liberally. For Presbyterians, then, abortion is no more a moral "right" than is war. Such a *presumption* about preserving and protecting "all life" — and hence a moral presumption against abortion even when fetal "humanity" is in doubt — is completely absent from the RCRC literature.

In 1997, the 209th General Assembly voted to admonish strongly against "partial-birth" abortion procedures: "the procedure known as intact dilation and extraction (commonly called 'partial birth' abortion) of a baby who could live outside the womb is of grave moral concern and should be considered only if the mother's physical life is endangered by the pregnancy."[117] Although in 2002 this position was reinterpreted and the acceptable conditions expanded, even this change is formally part of a "just-abortion" rather than a "holy-abortion" framework:

> The ending of a pregnancy after the point of fetal viability is a *matter of grave moral concern* to us all, and may be undertaken only in the *rarest of circumstances and after prayer and/or pastoral care*, when necessary to save the life of a woman, to preserve the woman's health in circumstances of a serious risk to the woman's health, to avoid fetal suffering as a result of untreatable life-threatening medical anomalies, or in cases of incest or rape.[118]

As for sexuality more generally, the PC(USA) officially holds to the principles of sexual faithfulness in marriage and chastity outside of marriage. The Second Helvetic Confession, which is part of the authoritative tradition of the PC(USA)'s *Book of Confessions*, decries an "impure single life" and "fornications." The *Confession of 1967* states that "[a]narchy in sexual relationships is a symptom of man's alienation from God, his neighbor, and himself."[119] In 1998, the General Assembly issued a statement on youth sexuality that said, in part, that the church "affirm[s] to the youth of our denomination the good purpose and blessing of God in the *expression of sexuality within the bonds of marriage*."[120] It called on churches, youth leaders, and families to teach "sexual purity in relation to Christian discipleship" and insure that all youth curricula and activities "conform to the biblical and constitutional standards of the PC(USA) regarding sexual behavior." This affirmation would make it inappropriate for a PC(USA) church to use RCRC materials — which do not advocate abstinence outside of marriage — with its youth, or to commend RCRC activities.

To summarize, the PC(USA) restricts sex to marriage, sees all life as precious to God, rejects abortion as birth control or for convenience or embarrassment, and accepts abortion only as a last resort and under certain conditions. This is not at all the moral position of RCRC.

The Episcopal Church (USA)

The Episcopal Church (USA), or ECUSA, maintains ties to RCRC through the offices of Women for Social Witness and Women in Mission and Ministry. Does this affiliation make sense in light of the church's perspective on abortion?

The most recent comprehensive statement on abortion from the Episcopal Church (USA) was issued by the denomination's 69th General Convention in 1988. At its 71st General Convention in 1994, the Episcopal Church reaffirmed the 1988 statement (with one minor modification). It also added a paragraph interpreting the 1988 statement's call for respect for "individual conscience" in the legal realm as "unequivocal opposition" to any governmental restriction of a woman's right to abort.[121]

The 1988/1994 statement reads, in part:

> *All human life is sacred from its inception* until death. [1988: "All human life is sacred. Hence, it is sacred from its inception until death."] The Church takes seriously its obligation to help form the consciences of its members concerning this *sacredness*. Human life, therefore, should be initiated only advisedly and in full accord with this understanding of the power to conceive and give birth which is bestowed by God....
>
> While we acknowledge that in this country it is the legal right of every woman to have a medically safe abortion, as Christians we believe strongly that if this right is exercised, it should be used *only in extreme situations*. We emphatically *oppose abortion as a means of birth control, family planning, sex selection, or any reason of mere convenience.*

In those cases where an abortion is being considered, members of this Church are urged to seek the dictates of their conscience in prayer, to **seek the advice and counsel of members of the Christian community** and where appropriate, the sacramental life of this Church....

Whenever members of this Church are consulted with regard to a problem pregnancy, they are to explore, with grave seriousness, with the person or persons seeking advice and counsel, as **alternatives to abortion**, other possible courses of action.... It is the responsibility of members of this Church, especially the clergy, to become aware of local agencies and resources which will **assist those faced with problem pregnancies**....[122]

Once again, we find a church that, despite its concurrence with RCRC's legal stance, espouses theological and ethical positions in stark contrast to those of RCRC. The Episcopal Church affirms the sacredness of human life from "inception." It justifies abortion only in "extreme situations," not as birth control, for family planning, for gender selection, or as a convenience. It requires Episcopalians to counsel pregnant women away from abortion and toward alternatives. Although the language of "last resort" is not explicitly used, the strong presumption against abortion and the condemnation of many common reasons for abortion imply a view of it only as a measure of last resort, subject to strict criteria. Finally, the church urges decision making within the Christian community.

Like the Methodists and the Presbyterians, then, the Episcopalians address abortion within the framework of the just-war tradition applied to this issue. Theologically and ethically speaking, abortion is not a moral right, much less a holy act, and it is not to be chosen in isolation.

A 1982 resolution strongly condemning abortion for non-serious fetal abnormalities (as well as gender selection) does not reappear in the 1988 statement but nonetheless remains the church's official position.[123] This further defines the criteria for ethical abortion, in harmony with a limited just-abortion approach.

The Episcopal Church has issued a few additional brief resolutions about abortion since 1988. All of these focus on or include relevant forms of ministry. In 1994, the General Convention commended and encouraged the work of its members in "pregnancy care centers" because they helped to fulfill the 1988 statement's commitment to "assist those faced with problem pregnancy."[124] Such centers were noted for their "**unconditional love and acceptance, for women and their unborn children.**" RCRC makes no similar commendations but instead labels such ministries "anti-choice" and accuses them of practicing dishonesty and offering "misinformation."[125]

In 2000, the General Convention called for the church to "embrace and minister to men and women who have participated in an abortion and who may feel the need for pastoral and sacramental ministries." It also urged parishes to become "safe communities" for the discussion of post-abortion stress.[126] In 1997, the Episcopal Church had expressed "grave concern" about partial-birth abortion and once again urged parishes to provide aid to pregnant women, implicitly as an alternative to seeking late abortion.[127]

On the issue of sexual relations, the same 1997 General Convention called on Episcopal parishes to "teach and support sexual abstinence" in its youth work.[128] One year later, the worldwide Anglican communion re-affirmed abstinence for all who are not called to marriage.[129]

Like the UMC and the PC(USA), the ECUSA is a church reluctant to approve abortion because it acknowledges and respects God's gift of life. Its theology of last resort, commitment to ethical criteria, and preference for abortion alternatives are all at odds with RCRC.

The United Church of Christ

The polity (church government) of the United Church of Christ (UCC) does not allow any one body to speak for any local congregation. In 1971, however, the General Synod of the United Church of Christ began a tradition of affirming "Freedom of Choice Concerning Abortion" (the title of its statement). It has reaffirmed freedom of choice on seven occasions since 1971 (most recently in 1991), including an extended and important 1987 statement called "Sexuality and Abortion: A Faithful Response."[130]

The United Church of Christ is perhaps, philosophically, RCRC's most ardent Christian affiliate. Until a recent re-organization, three denominational offices — the Board for Homeland Ministries, the Coordinating Center for Women, and the Office for Church in Society — expressed the UCC's support of RCRC through membership. Membership continues today through the denomination's office of Justice and Witness Ministries. Nevertheless, like the other mainline Protestant denominations we have considered, the UCC senses a tension between two aspects of the Christian tradition: "Scripture teaches us that all human life is precious in God's sight and teaches the importance of personal moral freedom."[131] The 1987 statement recalls that the UCC has always recognized the "moral ambiguity" of abortion and urged that "*alternatives to abortion always be fully and carefully considered,*" even while pressing for the "legal availability of abortion."

The statement then begins a series of resolutions. The first one "*affirms the sacredness of all life, and the need to protect and defend human life in particular.*" That is, the General Synod makes a profound theological statement about all human life, even (the context implies) human life *in utero.* The third resolution "upholds the right of men and women to have access to adequately funded family planning services, and to safe, legal abortions as one [family-planning] option among others." Between these two resolutions lies this one:

> [The General Synod] encourages persons facing unplanned pregnancies *to consider giving birth and parenting the child, or releasing the child for adoption, before abortion.*

In other words, the UCC's 1987 General Synod advocates a principle of *last resort* even while maintaining a policy of free access.

Remarkably, then, the UCC's 1987 General Synod echoes two of the themes we have seen in the other three mainline Protestant denominations: the sacredness of human life, and abortion as a last resort. These principles (one theological, one ethical) are not as fully developed or as explicit, respectively, as we have seen elsewhere, but they are nonetheless present.

To be sure, in spite of these two affirmations, the General Synod did not wish to see legal choice restricted; the last 1987 resolution urges all parties in the UCC to "oppose actively legislation and amendments which seek to revoke or limit access to safe and legal abortions." Moreover, the statement urges "responsible approaches to sexual behavior" and does not explicitly advocate abstinence outside marriage. And it suggests that abortion is a matter of "social justice" and even implies that it is a legitimate form of (last-resort) "family planning" or birth control. These are very similar indeed to RCRC's positions. *Nevertheless, even in the case of the UCC General Synod, one cannot help but sense an official theological and ethical ethos that differs in spirit, at least partially, from that of RCRC.*

Although the UCC must clearly be understood to differ from the other three mainline Protestant churches we have examined, it shares enough in common that its clergy, laity, and churches owe it to themselves at least to re-examine the propriety of membership in a coalition that finds abortion to be "holy."

In the first decade after *Roe v. Wade*, the American Baptist Churches, USA espoused a strong pro-choice position and were affiliated with RCAR. It became clear, however, that American Baptists were actually divided on the abortion issue and that membership in RCAR was not representative of the diversity in the denomination with respect to either the moral or the legal status of abortion.

In 1986, therefore, the American Baptist Churches left RCAR and in 1988 adopted a statement that reflects the diversity in the churches.[132] Its current position is that of the 1988 statement. The statement acknowledged that "[g]enuine diversity of opinion threatens" the unity of the American Baptist Churches and that the division is especially visible in the question of "the proper witness of the church to the state," with positions ranging across the spectrum from support for legalized abortion to support for legal protection of the unborn.[133]

Despite this diversity, the American Baptist Churches were able to come together to "acknowledge life as a *sacred and gracious gift of God*," to "*oppose abortion as a primary means of birth control*," and to encourage those considering abortion to "*seek spiritual counsel*." Furthermore, they agreed to urge members to model "responsible sexuality in *accordance with biblical teaching*."

In other words, the American Baptist Churches are close in spirit to the statements of churches that remain affiliated with RCRC. The Baptists, however, honor the diversity of their membership by encouraging each member "to advocate for a public policy on abortion that reflects his or her beliefs," rather than misrepresent the churches by affiliating with an organization that does not reflect that diversity at all.

The Moravian Church

The Moravian Church, Northern Province joined RCAR in 1986 but withdrew its membership in 1990. The church joined to demonstrate its commitment to religious liberty and individual conscience, and to express the conviction that it should not be dogmatic about ethical issues that the Bible does not address. Specifically, it affiliated with RCAR "in order to oppose legislation which would make all abortions illegal."[134] It left because membership in RCAR had quickly become a divisive issue, recommending that its Standing Committee on Church and Society explore membership.[135] (The Committee affiliated for a while but is not now a member.) Even when the Province joined RCAR in 1986, its own position (which was a reaffirmation of a 1974 statement) was to some degree at odds, theologically, with RCAR. The Moravian Church affirmed

> its belief in the *sacredness of life and the quality of life*, its belief that abortion should *not be used as a method of birth control nor as a means of controlling population*, and its belief that abortion should not be taken lightly or *without thorough consideration of alternatives and professional counseling....*[136]

Furthermore, as early as 1974, the Moravians had resolved that although abortion in some instances could be a way of "bringing mercy to a difficult situation," it should only be pursued after *"all other possible alternatives"* are considered but are finally believed to lead to "greater destruction of human life and spirit."[137] This is clearly an expression of the principle of last resort.

In 1990, when the Province left RCAR, it recognized a denominational need "to seek deeper spiritual truths concerning social issues and not merely to be aligned with one side on the issue of abortion."[138] It prepared and distributed a study paper. Implicitly, it recognized its differences with RCAR. *Most importantly, because of the complexity of the abortion issue and the divisiveness of affiliation with RCAR, it prudently recognized the error of continued denominational membership even without abandoning its pro-choice position.* The Moravian Church's position is very similar to at least three of the remaining Protestant bodies affiliated with RCRC. It may be prudent for other denominations to follow the Moravians' example.

The Evangelical Lutheran Church in America

The Evangelical Lutheran Church in America (ELCA) was formed in 1988 through the merger of three Lutheran bodies. The ELCA has never been officially affiliated with RCAR/RCRC. In 1995, the ELCA Churchwide Assembly voted 778 to 101 against a motion to permit the church to cooperate with RCRC, on the basis of a committee recommendation saying that the organization's exclusively pro-choice objectives were not congruent with the church's position.[139] (However, the Lutheran Women's Caucus — not an official church body — is a member of RCRC.)

Many aspects of the ELCA's position echo those of the Methodists, Presbyterians, and Episcopalians — which remain affiliated with RCRC. The ELCA has a clear just-abortion statement. In 1991, only three years after the ELCA was formed by the merger of three Lutheran denominations, the fledgling church deliberately tried to steer a middle course on abortion. That statement remains the ELCA's official policy. It declares that a

> developing life in the womb does not have an absolute right to be born, *nor does a pregnant woman have an absolute right to terminate a pregnancy*. The concern for both the life of the woman and the developing life in her womb expresses a common commitment to life.[140]

While the ELCA urges women with "unintended pregnancies" to be "good stewards of life by making responsible decisions in light of" their existing relationships, the church also declares that *"[h]uman life in all phases of its development is God-given and, therefore, has intrinsic value, worth, and dignity."* Thus, "human beings are called to respect and care for the life that God gives."

Practically, this declaration means the following for the ELCA:

> Because we believe that God is the creator of life, the number of induced abortions is a *source of deep concern* to this church. We *mourn the loss of life* that God has created. The strong Christian presumption is to preserve and protect life. *Abortion ought to be an option only of last resort.*

Furthermore, it affirms, "Because of the Christian presumption to preserve and protect life, this church, *in most circumstances, encourages women with unintended pregnancies to continue the pregnancy*." It does permit abortion explicitly if the pregnancy threatens the woman's physical life, is due to rape or incest, or reveals extreme fetal abnormality. It opposes abortion once a fetus is sufficiently viable to survive *extra-utero*.

The ELCA also strongly advises persons who are considering abortion to seek guidance from clergy, family, and professionals.

While the ELCA does not *explicitly* condemn abortion for birth-control purposes (though it certainly implies condemnation of it), in 1991, when the issue was most recently discussed, a significant number of Churchwide Assembly delegates voted to oppose such use of abortion.[141] In addition, the ELCA promotes abstinence outside of marriage and admonishes those who are sexually active to take into consideration the consequences of their actions. The 1991 document affirms that the new church's position was that "[m]arriage is the appropriate context for sexual intercourse." This continues to be the position of the ELCA, whose Church Council in 1996 reaffirmed *"abstinence outside of marriage."*[142]

The ELCA's views on abortion and sexuality are clearly at odds with RCRC's philosophy and activity. The ELCA affirms that abortion is only an option of "last resort," and decisions are to be sought in communal contexts. It stresses the holiness of the human body, sex within a covenantal context, and sexual abstinence outside marriage. These principles are nearly identical to those of the mainline Methodist, Presbyterian, and Episcopal churches.

The difference, of course, is that the ELCA is not part of RCRC. The ELCA has acted faithfully according to its teaching: this Lutheran body has demonstrated an exemplary integrity in disassociating itself from an organization whose position contradicts its own theology and ethics. Even though the ELCA's policy with respect to the law does not support regulation or prohibition of abortions generally (only after "viability"),[143] it appears to recognize that RCRC does not and cannot speak for its grave concerns about abortion — concerns it especially shares with at least three of the four mainline Protestant denominations that remain affiliated with RCRC.

The Lutherans (the ELCA), Moravians, and American Baptists all recognize that RCRC does not represent their theological statements or their constituencies, in which there exists great diversity of opinion. Other churches should learn from these three.

Conclusion

As noted at the beginning of this section, the key theological and ethical themes we have found in the mainline Protestant church documents we have examined that do not appear in RCRC's own literature are:

- responsible, covenantal sex within marriage and abstinence outside of marriage;
- decision making in the context of Christian community;
- the sacredness of unborn human life; and
- a presumption against the termination of unborn human life, and abortion only as a reluctantly approved last resort, but never as a means of birth control.

Although the churches affiliated with RCRC have issued statements that differ markedly from the position of RCRC, we know of course that those official policies can be, and often are, interpreted very loosely. The result is that, in some cases, the churches' *official* (*de jure*) position and its *actual* (*de facto*) position — expressed in curricula, in sermons, in pastoral counseling settings, in denominational activities and affiliations — are not unified. In fact, these churches are sometimes filled, not with the spirit of abortion-as-last-resort, but with the spirit of abortion-as-right, the spirit of RCRC.

Nevertheless, according to their official documents, the mainline Protestant churches we have discussed are profoundly disturbed at the way in which abortion has become a form of birth control and is symptomatic of a widespread casual attitude about sex and about human life. (This has led some of the denominations not only to say that alternatives to abortion are preferable, but also to support ministries that actually provide alternatives to pregnant women and teens.) The literature of RCRC, however, manifests no such concern or spirit. Unfettered sexual and reproductive freedom is celebrated, not mourned.

Furthermore, it should be carefully noted that these denominational statements *never describe abortion as a holy activity or a work of God*. The silence of these statements in this regard speaks loudly. Unlike RCRC itself, its affiliated churches know better than to adopt a holy-war attitude toward abortion. They understand the Christian presumption against taking human life, even life *in utero*. They firmly believe that violating that principle can only be done as a last resort. They know that the God they worship does not sanction unfettered choice on such grave matters of life and death.

For these reasons, all entities of The United Methodist Church, the Presbyterian Church (USA), the Episcopal Church (USA), and the United Church of Christ — as well as all Christians who do not accept the holy-war position of RCRC on abortion — ought to demonstrate their integrity and their commitment to represent their own communities by disassociating from the Religious Coalition for Reproductive Choice.

As this disassociation occurs, these churches and Christians will once again need to grapple seriously with the issue of abortion. In the next part of this book, we seek to introduce fresh voices and perspectives into that renewed conversation.

IV. Advancing the Conversation

SO FAR IN THIS BOOK WE HAVE EXAMINED the position of RCRC and of some of its member denominations. We have concluded that despite a common commitment to the maintenance of abortion as a legal option, RCRC and its major affiliated Protestant denominations are fundamentally at odds on the theological significance of abortion. In this section, we seek to advance the conversation by briefly examining abortion theologically from yet another point of view. We build on the strengths of the various statements that differ from RCRC's position, but also move in a new direction. To do so, we will take up the six RCRC themes once again.

If the Christian tradition has rejected and must reject the holy-war tradition, it must not become complacent about the just-war tradition, as if in the matter of war and peace (or in the matter of abortion) that tradition were finalized for all time. For one thing, the just-war tradition itself has come under increasing scrutiny in many churches, and the non-violence of Jesus and Paul is becoming more and more the norm for many ethicists and theologians. For another, the Christian tradition of non-violence is especially relevant for the question of abortion, since the parallel between war and abortion is inherently problematic. Why? Because it is very difficult to argue that the embryo or fetus is normally an aggressor whose life can be justifiably ended. These two factors make it imperative for the mainline churches to look again at the consistency and appropriateness of their own just-war-type positions on abortion. Our argument below suggests that the Christian churches should not only reject the holy-abortion position of RCRC, but also move beyond the just-abortion theory of the mainline Protestant denominations affiliated with RCRC.

As in the previous two sections, some significant phrases are placed in boldface italic type.

1. Freedom, Rights, and Justice
Freedom and Rights
RCRC has a theology of near-absolute freedom of the self in the areas of sexuality and reproductive control. What is missing from RCRC's theology of freedom is any sense of the paradoxical character of human freedom that permeates Scripture: true freedom is loving obedience to God, an allegiance to and performance of the ways of God. From a biblical perspective, any other notion of freedom is, at best, a caricature of true freedom. As ELCA pastor-theologian Rev. Leonard Klein writes:

> [C]hoice, in and of itself, in the sense of liberty without commandment or attachment, law or accountability, is, as we

should already know, not part of the biblical message. After all, when people in the Bible choose, they often choose badly, sinfully. Therefore, we can see that "pro-choice" is no more a Christian virtue than "pro-Yankees."[144]

The great reformed theologian Karl Barth put the matter even more bluntly:

> The decisive point is whether freedom in the Christian sense is identical with the freedom of Hercules: choice between two ways in a crossroad. ***This is a heathen notion of freedom***. Is it freedom to decide for the devil?... Light is light and not darkness. If it shines, *darkness is done away with*, not proposed for a choice. Being a slave of Christ means being free.[145]

Moreover (and again paradoxically), for the biblical writers, freedom is not a *private* experience but a *communal* reality. It is known, not in the pursuit of self-interest, but in a life of self-giving for the good of others. This is the deepest conviction of both Paul and Jesus, and of the Christian Church when it is faithful.

RCRC contends that a woman alone has the right to decide the fate of the unborn (or "potential") life in her womb. To many, this sounds logical and natural, but a bit of historical perspective on this subject is illuminating. In the ancient world, it was believed that women, slaves, and children (born and unborn) were the property of men, and that the male head of the household had the power of life and death (in Latin, *patria potestas*) over them, especially over their slaves and children. The noted church historian Gerald Bonner therefore observes that in our day abortion "has been defended on the grounds of the freedom of the parent — though now it is the mother, not the father, who has the power of decision, the *patria potestas* of antiquity being superseded by a *potestas materna*."[146] The current RCRC perspective, then, is nothing other than a revival of Roman power, the domination of the powerful over the powerless and allegedly non-human. This perspective is part of a larger, cultural, structural sin — "a 'culture of death'" — that has been characterized as "*a war of the powerful against the weak*" and a "*conspiracy against life*."[147]

Some will of course argue that the embryo or fetus is a part of the woman's body, or perhaps an uninvited resident in her body. They will also argue that a woman (or man) has the right to use her (or his) body for sexual pleasure and the right not to be hindered from that by the threat of pregnancy. A truly Christian perspective, however, will not allow the secular notion of one's body as one's own possession to infiltrate Christian ethics. As Paul himself wrote (and we quoted above): "[D]o you not know that your body is a temple of the Holy Spirit within you, which you have from God, and that you are not your own? For you were bought with a price; therefore glorify God in your body" (1 Cor. 6:19-20).

The idea that one has some "right" to use one's body for sexual intimacy or to abort a human life, even if one calls it a "potential" human life, that resides within one's body violates this basic Pauline principle:

> St. Paul's perspective, that Christians belong not to themselves but to Another, is at the core of his entire Christian ethics and is echoed in various ways throughout the entire New Testament.... The New Testament perspective [on the human body] is... completely antithetical to the claim that there is a divinely granted right to engage in whatever form of sexual activity one prefers, or to choose an abortion because there is a divinely given gift of freedom to do with one's body whatever one wishes to do. For Paul and the New Testament generally, this is not freedom but slavery. *The Pauline/New Testament perspective, therefore, challenges two of the dominant cultural values of our day that have too often been absorbed and advocated by spokespersons for the church — virtually unlimited sexual and procreative freedom*.[148]

In their provocative book *Not My Own: Abortion and the Marks of the Church*, Terry Schlossberg (a Presbyterian elder) and the late Elizabeth Achtemeier (a Presbyterian biblical scholar) argue that the "Christian Church is the instrument God has chosen to proclaim the glad news that we are not our own!"[149] "We are not," they aver, "lonely, isolated, self-enclosed little egos, turned in upon ourselves, whose neighbors and whose unborn children are but an obstacle to our own self-fulfillment."[150] Furthermore, *"the Christian can never say with those who support abortion, 'My body is my own.'"*[151] Even an advocate of just abortions rightly says that the commonly held pro-choice position "might better be labeled *pro-self*."[152]

The RCRC is, then, a misguided and unbiblical representative of the churches. Its message is one of what ethicists might call radical ethical egoism, or self-interest. Although many of the affiliated churches' statements contain challenges to RCRC's views, those views are thoroughly entrenched in American culture and, unfortunately, in many of the Christian churches, even within their leadership. Therefore,

> [t]he greatest challenge to commonly held beliefs, both within and beyond the church, will be to convince both men and women that they have *no absolute right over their own bodies, and absolutely*

no right over the lives and bodies of others.... Nothing short of radical conversion from these reincarnations of Roman power over women [by men] and the unborn [by women] will alter the current situation. This conversion, like divine judgment, must begin with the household of God.[153]

The freedom-of-choice movement, both secular and religious, promised liberation to women. Many women who have followed the movement's counsel have found oppression and grief rather than liberation and joy. They are now suffering the sad and difficult consequences of their decisions, and seeking pastoral care and divine healing. Some parts of the Church are finally recognizing their obligations to such women — and often the men in their lives, too. So far, however, many post-abortive women tell us, there has been little liberation or justice.

Justice
RCRC, as we noted, has much to say about rights for women and minorities. But in an important essay called "Using the Bible in the Debate about Abortion," University of Sheffield professor of biblical studies J.W. Rogerson, who is also an Anglican priest, contends that the discussion of rights and justice from a biblical perspective must recognize that the fundamental word of Scripture "about minorities and the defenceless... [is] 'the strong must defend the weak.'" To apply this biblical imperative today, he writes,

> *we must include the unborn among the weak and defenceless....*
> They are as much in need of defence as are people who are wrongly imprisoned and are as easily eradicated from our consciences... [for] we have become tolerant of the destruction and cheapening of human lives in many ways (including plans for future so-called nuclear defence.)[154]

A biblically informed theology of freedom, rights, and justice will not pit women's freedom and rights over against the life of the unborn. There must be a both-and solution, rather than an either-or solution, if we are to remain faithful to the biblical mandate.

2. The Role of Community
RCRC is so completely preoccupied with individual rights, and with a vision of justice that above all enhances those individual rights, that it fails to present any biblically or theologically shaped vision of religious life in community. That is, it has no vision of the Church. This deficiency is

inexcusable in a day when the Christian churches are fighting the battle against Western individualism and privatism on every imaginable front, and when the issue of the identity and mission of the Church in its culture is one of the most significant theological conversations taking place.

Hospitality
Stanley Hauerwas, the distinguished United Methodist theological ethicist who is one of the leading voices in this conversation about the Church in a post-Christian culture, writes about its impact on the abortion issue:

> All my work on abortion is based on this premise: you cannot separate the act called abortion from the kind of people and virtues that create the description of that action. For the Church, abortion is a description with which we remind ourselves of the virtues we should have as a Christian people — and that especially includes *hospitality* [to one another and to the stranger], *the readiness to welcome new life among us*, to the point of challenging the way we live.[155]

He admonishes the Church to listen to itself:

> Listen to the [Church's] baptismal vows; in them the whole Church promises to be parent. In this regard the Church reinvents the family.... The Church is a family into which children are brought and received. It is only within that context that it makes sense for the Church to say, "We are always ready to receive children." *The People of God know no enemy when it comes to children*.[156]

Presbyterian (PCUSA) minister Rev. Terry Hamilton-Poore argues that the Christian response to abortion

> centers on the responsibility of the whole Christian community to care for "the least of these," which is a manifestation of the commitment a congregation makes to new members in such liturgies as that of the Presbyterian Church's *Book of Order* (to which there are many parallels) when it responds affirmatively to the question, "Do you, the members of this congregation, in the name of the whole Church of Christ, undertake the responsibility for the continued Christian nurture of this person....?"[157]

Hauerwas applauds this sermon because it "suggests [rightly] that abortion is not a question about the law, but about what kind of people we are to be as the Church and as Christians."[158] This is why the Episcopal Church, as noted in section III, has rightly commended and encouraged the ministry of "pregnancy care centers." But this kind of ministry needs to become the ministry of the entire Christian Church. Schlossberg and Achtemeier therefore echo Hamilton-Poore, maintaining that another liturgical rite, baptism, "lays upon the [whole] church the responsibility for welcoming, rather than aborting, its children."[159]

Imagination and Action
There can be little doubt that it will take a rearrangement of our ecclesial mindsets to become the hospitable community Scripture calls the Church to be. It will be a great challenge

> to the moral life of the Church and its various institutions... ***to find the imagination and will to become channels of life and grace***, where the "orphan and the widow" are welcome. This life will be ***dedicated not only to rescuing the unborn from death but also to improving the quality of life for women and children.***[160]

RCRC literature sometimes caricatures pro-life people not only as "anti-choice" but as dangerously single-minded:

> Meanwhile those somebodies who claim they're "pro-life" aren't moved to help the living. They're not out there fighting to break the stranglehold of drugs and violence in our communities, trying to save our children, or moving to provide infant and maternal nutrition and health programs. Eradicating our poverty isn't on their agenda. No — somebody's too busy picketing, vandalizing and sometimes bombing family planning clinics, harassing women, and denying funds to poor women seeking abortions.[161]

Despite the inaccurate and unfair caricature presented in this text, it reminds the entire Christian Church that it must be a community that does not allow itself to choose between women and children. The cry of the poor and oppressed cannot go unheeded, but neither can it be answered with further oppression and violence of any sort, including abortion. That is not Christian mercy.

The prominent New Testament theologian Richard Hays, who is ordained in The United Methodist Church and teaches at Duke, provocatively suggests that the liberal Protestant church's advocacy of abortions for poor women who cannot afford to raise children is a tragic symbol that the church has lost its vision for communal sharing and consequently acquiesced to the power of death. The church's confusion on the issue of abortion is a *symptom* of its more fundamental unfaithfulness to the economic imperatives of the gospel.[162]

Addressing all churches and Christians, Hays contends that

within the church, there should be no justification for abortion on economic grounds or on the ground of the incapacity of the mother to care for the child.... Sharing, not abortion, is the answer. That is what it means to live out the power of the resurrection.[163]

3. The Status of the Fetus

RCRC consistently asserts that the embryo or fetus is not, and is not to be considered, a human being or a person who possesses rights or to whom we have any obligations. The lack of theological, biblical, and philosophical sophistication in these assertions cannot be addressed in the space we have. Rather, we will make three major points about this crucial matter.

The Meaning of Personhood

First, a strong case has been made by Oxford's Regius Professor of Moral and Pastoral Theology, Oliver O'Donovan (an Anglican clergyman), that unborn children can and ought to be recognized as persons by Christians. "Personhood," he argues persuasively, is not an objective status attained by the possession of certain biological or other criteria. Rather, drawing inspiration from the parable of the Good Samaritan, O'Donovan demonstrates that personhood (or "humanity") is something we *discover* only in the reciprocal process of engaging the other as person and of our being engaged as person by that other. In that process, we discover the personhood, not only of the other, but of ourselves.[164] To borrow the closing thought of Jesus' parable, *in recognizing the unborn child as our neighbor, we become the neighbor God wills for us to be*.

Richard Hays, also commenting on the parable of the Good Samaritan, writes in the same vein that

the point is that we are called upon to *become* neighbors... [both] to the mother in a "crisis pregnancy" and to her unborn child.... To define the unborn child as a nonperson is to narrow the scope of moral concern, whereas Jesus calls upon us to widen it by showing mercy and actively intervening on behalf of the helpless. The Samaritan is a paradigm of the love that goes beyond ordinary obligation and thus *creates* a neighbor relation where none existed before.[165]

The Christian Tradition

Second, as noted earlier, the Christian Church was born into a pagan culture in which the non-humanity or non-personhood of the unborn (not to mention women, already-born children, and slaves) was taken for granted. Christianity both implicitly and explicitly challenged this cultural assumption. For instance:

- the early church documents called the *Didache* (ca. 96) and *The Epistle of Barnabas* (ca. 135) included abortion as one of the sins that violated the command to love one's neighbor as, or more than, oneself;
- the second-century apologist Athenagoras said that the fetus is "the object of God's care"; and
- the late-second/early-third century theologian Tertullian argued that abortion is "merely a speedier homicide."

Similar statements are found throughout early Christian literature as part of the early church's "humanization" or "neighborization" of the Roman empire's non-persons.[166]

Third, both RCRC as an organization and its various contributors are completely out of step with the Christian tradition on the status of unborn human life. In the Christian tradition, the unborn human (i.e., the embryo and fetus) is the special creation of God that is to be treated with dignity and respect; it is deserving of care and protection by those already born.

This tradition is ably summarized in "A Theologians' Brief: On the Place of the Human Embryo within the Christian Tradition and the Theological Principles for Evaluating its Moral Status," a document written for presentation to the British House of Lords Select Committee on Stem Cell Research in 2001.[167] It is signed, not by ideologues with a common agenda, but by an *ad hoc* ecumenical group of distinguished theologians who have independently arrived at the same conclusions. The Protestant, Anglican, Catholic, and Orthodox signers include the new Archbishop of Canterbury, Rowan Williams; the leading Orthodox theologian, Kallistos Ware; Anglican ethicist and Oxford professor Oliver O'Donovan; Lutheran ethicist Gilbert Meilaender; Anglican theologian of radical orthodoxy John Milbank; Dominican scholar Aidan Nichols; and leading classicist John Rist.[168]

A substantive set of excerpts from their very important statement follows:

In asserting that 'life must be protected with the utmost care from conception' [Second Vatican Council, *Gaudium et Spes* 51] and rejecting 'the killing of a life already conceived' [Lambeth Conference 1958 report 'The Family in Contemporary Society' in *What the Bishops Have Said about Marriage*, London: SPCK, 1968, p. 17] twentieth century Christians were in continuity with the ***belief of the Early Church that all human life is sacred from conception***. This had remained a constant feature of Christian tradition despite a variety of beliefs about the origin of the soul and a similar variety in what legal penalties were thought appropriate for early or late abortion. In the tradition, the only precedents for attributing a 'graded status and protection' to the embryo can be found in the speculations of some of the Roman Catholic laxists of the seventeenth century and the re-emergence of similar and even more radical views among some Protestant and Roman Catholic writers in the late twentieth century. ***The great weight of the tradition, East and West, Orthodox, Catholic and Reformed, from the apostolic age until the twentieth century, is firmly against any sacrifice or destructive use of the early human embryo save, perhaps, 'at the dictate of strict and undeniable medical necessity'; that is, in the context of seeking to save the mother's life....***

For a Christian, the question of the status of the human embryo is directly related to the mystery of creation. In the context of the creation of things 'seen and unseen' the human being appears as the *microcosm*, reflecting in the unity of a single creature both spiritual and corporeal realities. The beginning of each human being is therefore a reflection of the coming to be of the world as a whole. It reveals the creative act of God bringing about the reality of *this* person (of me), in an analogous way to the creation of the entire cosmos. There is a mystery involved in the existence of each person.... Often in the Scriptures the forming of the child in the womb is described in ways that echo the formation of Adam from the dust of the earth. This is why Psalm 139 describes the child in the womb as being formed 'in the depths of the earth'. ***The formation of the human embryo is archetypal of the mysterious works of God.*** A passage that is significant for uncovering the connections between Genesis and embryogenesis is found in the deutero-canonical book of Maccabees, in a mother's speech to her son: 'I do not know how you came into being in my womb. It was not I who gave you life and breath, nor I who set in order the elements within each of you. Therefore the Creator of the world, who shaped the beginning of man and devised the origin of all things, will in his mercy give life and breath back to you again.'...

[T]he ambiguity in the appearance of the embryo has never been thought of as taking the embryo out of the realm of the human, the God-made and the holy. When Pope John Paul II asks, 'how can a human individual not be a human person?' [*Evangelium Vitae* (Gospel of Life) 60] he is not denying the mysteriousness of the implied answer. Christians recognize *the embryo to be sacred precisely because it is inseparable from the mystery of the creation of the human person by God. What is clear, at the very least, is that the embryo is 'a living thing — under the care of God'.* The following, then, are five principal considerations which should inform any Christian evaluation of the moral status of the human embryo:

I. Though penalties have varied, the Christian tradition has always extended the principle of the *sacredness of human life to the very beginning of each human being*, and *never allowed the deliberate destruction* of the fruit of conception.

II. The origin of each human being is *not only a work of nature but is a special work of God* in which God is involved from the very beginning.

III. The Christian doctrine of the soul is not dualistic but requires one to believe that, *where there is a living human individual, there is a spiritual soul.*

IV. Each human being is *called and consecrated by God in the womb from the first moment of his or her existence*, before he or she becomes aware of it. Traditionally, Christians have expressed the human need for redemption as extending from the moment of conception.

V. *Jesus*, who reveals to Christians what it is to be human, was a *human individual from the moment of his conception*, celebrated

on the feast of the Annunciation, nine months before the feast of
Christmas....

The above assertions apply also, of course, to the fetus as well as the
embryo.

The Unborn as Work of God and Moral "Other"

For Christians who value their shared history and most fundamental
common convictions that reach across time and traditions, then, the status
of the human embryo and fetus can be affirmed as nothing less than a
"special work of God in which God is involved from the very beginning."
Therefore, in the words of the new Archbishop of Canterbury, Rowan
Williams (a life member of Britain's Society for the Protection of Unborn
Children[169]), *"from the moment of conception there is a moral other
involved"*; the "unborn," like the "handicapped," are a group of "people
whose needs or claims we [think we] can safely ignore." Abortion, he
contends in continuity with Christian tradition, "is taking human life."[170]

In a similar vein, the prominent German theologian Jürgen
Moltmann reminds us of the consequences of failing to recognize the
dignity of the human person from conception on:

> *Every devaluation of the fetus, the embryo, and the fertilized
> ovum compared with life that is already born and adult is the
> beginning of a rejection and a de-humanization of human
> beings.* Hope for the resurrection of the body does not permit any
> such death sentence to be passed on life. Fundamentally speaking,
> human beings mutilate themselves when embryos are devalued into
> mere "human material," for *every human being was once just
> such an embryo in need of protection.*[171]

There may remain in certain quarters some quibbling about the
exact language with which to describe this "special work." Dietrich
Bonhoeffer, however, speaks to and for the greater Church in dismissing
this quibbling as grounds for support of abortion:

> Destruction in the mother's womb is a violation of the right to live
> which God has bestowed upon this nascent life. To raise the
> question whether we are here concerned already with a human
> being or not is merely to confuse the issue. *The simple fact is that
> God certainly intended to create a human being and that this
> nascent human being has been deliberately deprived of his life.*
> And that is nothing but murder.[172]

This is hardly the position of RCRC. Some of its affiliated churches, however, are finally at least approaching congruence with the Christian tradition. It is time for them to move still closer to their heritage.

4-5. Abortion as Birth Control and as Holy Act

As we have seen, RCRC supports abortion as a legitimate form of birth control and, indeed, as a holy act. But if the preceding discussion, including especially the theological statement cited in the last section, is correct, then the response to RCRC's position must be the following: ***It is an historical and theological anomaly of the most serious kind for Christian people to consider the regular practice of abortion as something moral, just, or holy.***

This conclusion is predicated on the arguments in sections 1-3 and in 6 below, and will not be developed in depth here. The burden of proof, however, is on those who would conclude otherwise.

6. The Character of the God Attested in Scripture

RCRC is fond of highlighting the biblical theme of freedom and choice (though its interpretation of this theme is subject to question) and attributing to God a "pro-choice" nature. Part of RCRC's argument is the "silence" of the Bible on the subject of abortion. But RCRC neglects biblical themes other than freedom and choice in the construction of its deity.

For instance, John Rogerson agrees with RCRC that the Bible does not address abortion directly. Rather, Rogerson argues, what the Bible does is "to ask us whether at one and the same time we can assert our faith in a God who seeks the unworthy and the unwanted, and be indifferent to the fact that thousands of unwanted unborn children have their individuality terminated."[173]

Rogerson produces several pieces of evidence that suggest that "abortion was not commonly practised, if at all, in ancient Israel."[174] It is well known by historians that in the Hellenistic and Roman periods (including the time of Jesus and Paul) Jews distinguished themselves from Gentiles by not practicing abortion, infanticide, or the exposure of newborns, and that this was part of their ethic of love, justice, and hospitality.[175] This ethic continued in the early church, for as the distinguished patristics scholar Gerald Bonner has written, the prohibition of abortion was "the universal teaching of the early Church."[176] The "silence" of the New Testament on abortion must not be understood as evidence for early Christian acceptance of the practice — which would be a complete contradiction of everything we know about the earliest Christians' parent (Judaism) and child (post-apostolic Christianity) — but

59

as an historical accident that occurred as the New Testament canon developed over several centuries.[177]

Richard Hays suggests that the silence of the New Testament on abortion necessitates our "placing the problem in the broader framework of the New Testament's *symbolic world* and then reflecting analogically about the way in which the New Testament might provide implicit *paradigms* for our response to the question." When we do so, he argues, we find that to "terminate a pregnancy is not only to commit an act of violence but also to assume responsibility for destroying a work of God... to dispose of life that does not belong to us" — whether or not we call the unborn child a "person," Hays insists.[178]

We cannot conclude, therefore, that the God of the Scriptures is a "pro-choice" God who permits or sanctifies abortion. Rather, Jews and Christians who first read their Scriptures in an abortion culture found God calling them to oppose it as a practice unfit for God's holy people. And it is unfit for God's holy people in part because it does not reflect the holy and loving character of God. As the Church of the Brethren, speaking as one of the historic peace churches, said in 1984, the Church "opposes abortion because the rejection of unborn children violates the love by which God creates and nurtures human life."[179]

V. Conclusions and Possible Objections

IN THIS BOOK WE HAVE EXAMINED the mission of the Religious Coalition for Reproductive Choice and various RCRC materials that present its position on abortion and related issues. We have compared and contrasted this position with the official statements of mainline Protestant denominations that have some formal affiliation with RCRC. And we have attempted to advance the conversation about abortion by providing significant theological perspectives on the subject that are neglected by RCRC. Throughout the book we have argued that the fundamental theological and ethical differences between RCRC and most mainline Protestant denominations render the affiliation of these denominations and their members with RCRC inappropriate. They are "unequally yoked," and it is time for the relationship to end.

Our primary thesis has been that RCRC espouses a position that makes abortion the moral equivalent of holy war. That is, RCRC presents abortion as the sacred, divinely given and sanctioned right of sovereign, isolated moral agents to practice, even as birth control, without legal restraint of any kind, without concern about the moral status of the embryo or fetus, and without any moral guidelines other than their own, internalized, pro-choice morality/deity. In contrast, we have shown, the basic mainline Protestant position on abortion is akin to the just-war theory in permitting abortion only as a last resort, never as a means of birth control or for convenience, only with due respect for the sacredness of unborn human life as God's gift, and only within a Christian community's guidelines.

Because RCRC and its affiliated mainline denominations concur on the proposition that abortion should be legal, it would be easy to miss the radical difference between these two positions:

The RCRC position *absolutizes, sanctifies,* and even *deifies choice,* but it *dehumanizes human life before birth*, while the mainline position maintains the *sacredness of human life even before birth* and *relativizes the value of choice by setting parameters* for how choice is used.

The RCRC position proclaims, *"Abortion is holy because God is pro-choice,"* while the mainline position proclaims, *"Abortion is tragic because God is the giver of life."*

These two positions, we have argued, cannot co-exist. The RCRC view should be judged no less inherently inappropriate, and no less idolatrous and heretical, than the holy-war position itself.

Our secondary thesis has been that the Christian churches have historically had, and once again should have, a view of abortion that is even more radically different from RCRC's position than is the mainline Protestant view. The existence of fundamental differences from RCRC in the mainline position statements suggests that the Christian churches may be ready to re-consider abortion from the perspective of respected, ecumenical theological voices that RCRC completely avoids or misrepresents. Thus we have re-examined all of RCRC's major tenets in conversation with leading ecumenical theologians who espouse the Christian Church's treatment, through the ages, of the human embryo/fetus as a divine creation and a person to whom we have sacred obligations. This perspective has been placed within a larger worldview that holds that the Christian's supreme value is not choice but covenantal faithfulness to God, and that the Church is called to be a community of hospitality that welcomes both women in need and children *in utero*.

In sum, then, the Religious Coalition for Reproductive Choice and the Christian churches are unequally yoked. Abortion is *not* a holy act. RCRC does *not* represent the Christian faith in the matter of abortion. The Clergy for Choice Network is *not* an appropriate expression of Christian ministry. RCRC's youth associations and curricula perpetuate cultural norms that are *at odds* with the teachings of the Christian churches. In fact, RCRC and its subsidiaries have *betrayed* the Christian faith, its people, and its churches.

Possible Objections

We anticipate, and here briefly respond to, six possible major objections to our argument.

(1) Some may say that the real problem is not RCRC but its worship resource, *Prayerfully Pro-Choice*. We have shown, however, that this resource is vintage RCRC material, not an aberration. It is a window into RCRC's soul. *Lex orandi, lex credendi.*

(2) Others may contend that RCRC never explicitly states that abortion is a legitimate form of birth control. We have argued, however, that approving of abortion without ethical criteria and arguing for a right to terminate any unplanned pregnancy amount to treating abortion as a means of birth control.

(3) Still others may complain that RCRC never explicitly calls abortion "holy"; at most it views the *choice* for abortion as sacred. But

RCRC does explicitly claim that abortion providers do God's work and that abortion can accomplish God's will (however God is defined). RCRC does speak of divine sanction and blessing through abortion, not merely in the decision-making process. This is what "holy" means. Moreover, we have demonstrated that RCRC's position is parallel in many ways to the holy-war tradition, and there are certainly situations in which holy warriors use much God-talk to justify their activity without explicitly calling their warfare "holy." A rose by any other name....

(4) Some may argue that the differences between RCRC and the mainline Protestant churches are minor matters and that they agree on the major issue: keeping abortion legal. This attitude, however, fails to recognize that for the Church, theological and ethical issues are the foundational matters, while legal concerns are derivative. We have shown that the agreement between RCRC and its affiliated churches about the law is actually a superficial accord because the theological and ethical differences between RCRC and those same churches are so profound.

(5) Yet others may suggest that we are proposing the imposition of one narrow perspective on the Christian churches, and perhaps also on the entire country. Quite the contrary, we would argue: it is RCRC that espouses a narrow, holy-abortion theological perspective that represents neither the churches' official just-abortion positions nor the diversity of actual positions within their memberships.

(6) Finally, some may suspect that ultimately this book is not about ending membership in RCRC but about reversing *Roe v. Wade*. This is simply not true. We believe that the Church needs to get its own house in order. There is no doubt, however, that reopening the theological, ethical, and pastoral dimensions of the abortion problem will eventually lead to a reconsideration of legal issues. But we will let that discussion unfold over time.

It is our conviction that none of these possible objections can be sustained, and that the argument of this book is persuasive. The relationship between RCRC and mainline Protestant Christians is inappropriate. It is time for this relationship to end, and for Christian lay people, clergy, churches, and denominations to pursue a more appropriate and truly Christian response to the problem of abortion.

As WE COMPLETE THE WRITING OF THIS SMALL BOOK in early 2003, we are witnesses to what is perhaps a unique ecumenical moment in recent history: the nearly unanimous voice of the Christian churches — not only in the U.S. but around the world — in opposition to a hurried, unjust war. Some oppose this war because of opposition to all wars; some find this war unjustified according to the Christian just-war tradition; many in both groups see an unhealthy, almost holy-war mentality proceeding from some who seek to prosecute the war.

What all of us, as Christians, believe is that we must have a very strong, and perhaps absolute, presumption *against* the taking of human life and *for* the protecting of human life. In our present global context, we are learning once again that pursuing violence is not the appropriate Christian way to seek justice. Violence only perpetuates violence; death promotes death, not life.

The united witness of the Christian churches in this regard is not merely unusual; it is exemplary. That is, it is exemplary *for us*. Just as the Christian churches are one in trying to pursue justice, order, and peace without war, so also — perhaps — we can now creatively seek justice and mercy for women without practicing violence and injustice toward other members of the human family created by God. We are fully aware, of course, that the Church's witness will not stop all war (and perhaps not even this war) or end all abortions. But if we can come together to preach and practice imaginative alternatives to violence, we will indeed see more fully both the unity of the Church for which the Lord Jesus Christ prayed and the new creation that God inaugurated in Christ's birth, life, death, and resurrection. That is our fervent hope and prayer.

Appendix A: RCRC Member Bodies

(according to RCRC's website: www.rcrc.org/rcrc/members.htm)

CHRISTIAN

THE EPISCOPAL CHURCH

PRESBYTERIAN CHURCH (USA)
Women's Ministries, Washington
    Office

UNITED CHURCH OF CHRIST
Justice and Witness Ministries

UNITED METHODIST CHURCH
General Board of Church and Society
General Board of Global Ministries:
    Women's Division

CAUCUSES/OTHER ORGANIZATIONS*
American Baptist Witness for Choice
Catholics for a Free Choice
Church of the Brethren Women's
    Caucus
Disciples for Choice
Episcopal Urban Caucus
Episcopal Women's Caucus
Lutheran Women's Caucus
Methodist Federation for Social Action
Presbyterians Affirming Reproductive
    Options
YWCA of the USA

JEWISH

CONSERVATIVE MOVEMENT
Rabbinical Assembly
United Synagogue of Conservative
    Judaism
Women's League for Conservative
    Judaism

*Many of the caucuses and
organizations bearing denominational
names are not official denominational
bodies.*

RECONSTRUCTIONIST MOVEMENT
Jewish Reconstructionist Federation

REFORM MOVEMENT
Central Conference of American
    Rabbis
North American Federation of Temple
    Youth
Union of American Hebrew
    Congregations
Women of Reform Judaism: The
    Federation of Temple Sisterhoods
Women's Rabbinic Network

ORGANIZATIONS
American Jewish Committee
American Jewish Congress
Anti-Defamation League of B'nai
    B'rith
Hadassah, WZOA
Jewish Women International
NA'AMAT USA
National Council of Jewish Women
Women's American ORT

**AMERICAN HUMANIST
ASSOCIATION**

**ETHICAL CULTURE
MOVEMENT**
American Ethical Union
National Service Conference of the
    American Ethical Union

UNITARIAN UNIVERSALIST
Unitarian Universalist Association
Unitarian Universalist Women's
    Federation
Young Religious Unitarian
    Universalists

Appendix B: For Further Reading

Channer, J.H., ed. *Abortion and the Sanctity of Human Life.* Exeter: Paternoster; Greenwood, S.C.: Attic, 1985. Essays by Gerald Bonner, Oliver O'Donovan, John Rogerson, and others.

Engelhardt, H. Tristram, Jr. *The Foundations of Christian Bioethics.* Lisse, Netherlands: Swets & Zeitlinger, 2000.

Gorman, Michael J. *Abortion and the Early Church: Christian, Pagan, and Jewish Attitudes in the Greco-Roman World.* Downers Grove, Ill.: InterVarsity; Mahwah, N.J.: Paulist, 1982; repr. Eugene, Ore.: Wipf & Stock, 1998.

_____. "Scripture, History, and Authority in a Christian View of Abortion: A Response to Paul Simmons." *Christian Bioethics* 2 (1996): 83-96.

Hays, Richard B. *The Moral Vision of the New Testament: A Contemporary Introduction to New Testament Ethics.* San Francisco: HarperSanFrancisco, 1996, chap. 18 (pp. 444-61).

John Paul II, Pope. *The Gospel of Life [Evangelium Vitae].* New York: Random House, 1995.

Jones, David, *et al.* "A Theologian's Brief: On the Place of the Human Embryo Within the Christian Tradition and the Theological Principles for Evaluating Its Moral Status." *Ethics & Medicine* 17/3 (Fall 2001): 143-54. Or see: www.linacre.org/atheol.html or www.ethicsandmedicine.com/17/3/17-3-jones.htm.

Schlossberg, Terry and Elizabeth Achtemeier. *Not My Own: Abortion and the Marks of the Church.* Grand Rapids: Eerdmans, 1995.

Stallsworth, Paul T., ed. *The Church and Abortion.* Nashville: Abingdon, 1993. Essays by Ruth Brown, Michael Gorman, Stanley Hauerwas, and William Willimon.

_____., ed. *Thinking Theologically about Abortion.* Anderson, Ind.: Bristol House, 2000. Essays by Elizabeth Achtemeier, Carl Braaten, Leonard Klein, and Richard John Neuhaus.

note: all URLs were verified and accurate as of December 1, 2002

1. Emphasis added to both quotations.

2. Stanley Hauerwas, "Abortion, Theologically Understood," in Paul T. Stallsworth, ed., *The Church and Abortion* (Nashville: Abingdon, 1993), p. 64.

3. The phrase in quotes is the title of an introductory brochure. The Religious Coalition for Reproductive Choice now has offices at 1025 Vermont Ave., NW, Suite 1130, Washington, DC 20005; phone 202-628-7700; web site: www.rcrc.org. It was formerly located in The United Methodist Building across from the Supreme Court.

4. See Appendix A for a list of these organizations.

5. Quoted in RCRC's 2000 Annual Report, p. 24, and elsewhere in RCRC literature.

6. The longer version is quoted from the pamphlet "Religious Coalition for Reproductive Choice: The Interfaith Movement for Choice," p. 1, and the shorter from RCRC's 2000 billboard advertising campaign, documented in its 2000 Annual Report, pp. 4-5.

7. See www.rcrc.org/rcrc/geninfo.html, "Our Vision." The other mottos cited appear regularly in RCRC literature, on RCRC signs and billboards, etc.

8. "The Interfaith Movement for Choice" brochure, p. 2.

9. *Faith&Choices* newsletter, Winter 2001, p. 1.

10. All entities of the American Baptist Churches, the Church of the Brethren, the Christian Church (Disciples of Christ), and the Moravian Church have disaffiliated from RCAR/RCRC in the last two decades.

11. All phrases in quotes are taken from RCRC's "The Interfaith Movement for Choice" brochure; emphasis added.

12. *Prayerfully Pro-Choice: Resources for Worship*, pp. 36-37; emphasis added.

13. For example: the Episcopal Church, in 1967; the United Methodist Church, in 1968, 1970, and 1972; the United Presbyterian Church, a predecessor of the Presbyterian Church (USA), and the American Friends Service Committee, in 1970; also, the National Federation of Temple Sisterhoods (Reform), in 1965, and the Central Conference of American Rabbis (Reform), in 1967; in addition, the Unitarian Universalist Association, in 1967.

14. For the formation and early history of RCAR, in addition to RCAR/RCRC literature, see Samuel A. Mills, "Abortion and Religious Freedom: The Religious Coalition for Abortion Rights (RCAR) and the Pro-choice Movement, 1973-1989," *Journal of Church of State* 33/3 (Summer 1991), which is also available online, with footnotes, at www.cgndesigns.com/passages/passages3.cfm?sortby=_author&urlFN=rcarabortion; and John H. Evans, "Multi-organizational Fields and Social Movement Organization Frame Content: The Religious Pro-Choice Movement," *Sociological Inquiry* 67/4 (Fall 1997), available online at:

www.princeton.edu/~sociolog/pdf/evans_95.pdf. See also the bibliographies included with these articles.

15. RCAR, "How We Stand," published in 1974.

16. Based on RCAR documents, Mills, "Abortion and Religious Freedom" (see the text near notes 2 and 84), claims that RCAR was a division of the United Methodist General Board of Church and Society until its independent incorporation in 1981, but we have been unable to corroborate this claim independently.

17. Evans, "Multi-organizational Fields," p. 8 [online .pdf version].

18. See Mills, "Abortion and Religious Freedom," and Evans, "Multi-organizational Fields."

19. Mills, "Abortion and Religious Freedom," text near notes 25-31. Brickner's view and interpretation of Judaism, it should be noted, are not accepted by all Jews, especially not by Orthodox Jews.

20. Mills, "Abortion and Religious Freedom," text near notes 32-43.

21. Mills, "Abortion and Religious Freedom," text near notes 94-99, documents a rise from 4,000 to 25,000 activists between 1978 and 1989.

22. Evans, "Multi-organizational Fields," pp. 12-15 [online .pdf version]. One of many results of this move, among evangelicals, was a book edited by Anne Eggebroten, *Abortion: My Choice, God's Grace; Christian Women Tell Their Stories* (Pasadena, Calif.: New Paradigm, 1994).

23. RCRC Annual Report 2000, p. 2; emphasis added.

24. "Religious Coalition Lobbies for Abortion, Gay Rights," NLJ Online; www.nljonline.com/September2000/coalition.htm, p. 2.

25. "Religious Coalition Lobbies for Abortion, Gay Rights," NLJ Online; www.nljonline.com/September2000/coalition.htm, p. 3.

26. In 2000, RCRC engaged Lake, Snell, Perry and Associates to poll national attitudes about religion and abortion.

27. Quotations are from the Spiritual Youth for Reproductive Freedom brochure; similarly, www.syrf.org, the home page of the group's website.

28. See www.feministcampus.org/spiritualityhouse.asp, accessible from www.syrf.org.

29. Described in the RCRC 2000 Annual Report, pp. 4-5.

30. RU-486 is used during the first seven weeks of a pregnancy, often in conjunction with a second drug; the two drugs cause the lining of a woman's uterus to shed, open the cervix, and start contractions that expel the embryo. See www.ru486facts.org.

31. See the description at http://www.rcrc.org/bci/keeping.html.

32. For a summary of RCRC activity on this issue, see Paul T. Stallsworth, "RCRC's Actions Speak Louder than its Words," *Lifewatch*, June 6, 2002, pp. 2-3; www.lifewatch.org/lifewatch060102.html.

33. See, for example, www.rcrc.org/new/legislativeissues.htm.

34. A 1998 membership appeal letter listed the Network membership at 4,000, but a recent inquiry to RCRC about current membership did not yield specific numbers.

35. Information and quotations are from the Clergy for Choice Network's invitational brochure and its website, www.rcrc.org/clergy.

36. All data in this section are found in the RCRC 2000 Annual Report, p. 22.

37. RCRC's 2000 Annual Report combines revenues from member bodies and affiliates.

38. See www.fordfound.org for details.

39. *Prayerfully Pro-Choice*, p. 3.

40. *Prayerfully Pro-Choice*, p. 64.

41. At www.syrf.org, this is listed as one of the goals of SYRF's "Spirituality House," which is SYRF's "virtual campus spirituality center."

42. RCRC, *We Remember*, p. 2.

43. RCRC, *Considering Abortion? Clarifying What You Believe*, p. 3; available at www.rcrc.org/religion/es9/es9.html.

44. See the description at http://www.rcrc.org/bci/keeping.html.

45. "For Some Teenagers, Abstinence is a Leap of Faith," Family Research Council: www.frc.org/get/cu01j1.cfm?CFID=72206&CFTOKEN=8343870#title2.

46. *Prayerfully Pro-Choice*, p. 10.

47. *Prayerfully Pro-Choice*, p. 9.

48. *Prayerfully Pro-Choice*, p. 86.

49. *Prayerfully Pro-Choice*, p. 42.

50. He is quoted or referenced, for example, by Rev. James Armstrong (*Prayerfully Pro-Choice*, p. 40) and by RCRC President and CEO Rev. Carlton W. Veazey (*Prayerfully Pro-Choice*, pp. 95-96).

51. "There was a time when the church was very powerful. It was during that period when the early Christians rejoiced when they were deemed worthy to suffer for what they believed. In those days the church was not merely a thermometer that recorded the ideas and principles of popular opinion; it was a thermostat that transformed the mores of society. Whenever the early Christians entered a town the power structure got disturbed and immediately sought to convict them for being 'disturbers of the peace' and 'outside agitators.' But they went on with the conviction that they were 'a colony of heaven,' and had to obey God rather than man. They were small in number but big in commitment. They were too God-intoxicated to be 'astronomically intimidated.' By their effort and example they brought an end to such ancient evils as infanticide and gladiatorial contest[s]" (*Letter from Birmingham City Jail*, pp. 289-302 in James Melvin Washington, ed. *A Testament of Hope: The Essential Writings of Martin Luther King, Jr.* [San Francisco: Harper & Row, 1986], here p. 300).

52. *Prayerfully Pro-Choice*, p. 95.

53. *Prayerfully Pro-Choice*, p. 66.

54. RCRC, *Considering Abortion? Clarifying What You Believe*, p. 4.

55. www.rcrc.org/rcrc/geninfo.html.

56. *Prayerfully Pro-Choice*, p. 11.

57. *Prayerfully Pro-Choice*, p. 41.

58. *Prayerfully Pro-Choice*, p. 41. We wish to note that Bishop Talbert has made significant contributions to ecumenical and (especially recently) peace efforts; we are asking for greater theological and moral consistency.

59. *Prayerfully Pro-Choice*, p. 117.

60. Available also at www.rcrc.org/religion/pamphlets/truth.html.

61. *Prayerfully Pro-Choice*, p. 81.

62. RCRC, *Black Ministers Support Your Right to Choose.*

63. Virginia Ramey Molenkott, "Respecting the Moral Agency of Women," p. 2; also at www.rcrc.org/religion/es1/full.html.

64. RCRC, *Barriers to Abortion are Barriers to Justice for Women*, p. 1. In September 2001, The Reverend Dr. Katherine Hancock Ragsdale, who is a member of the executive committee of RCRC, in testifying before a Congressional committee against the *Child Custody Protection Act*, advocated circumstances that would enable a minor to obtain an abortion without the involvement of her parents. She recommended that a "trusted adult" be permitted to serve as a parent substitute when a girl desires. See the testimony at www.rcrc.org/new/childbilltestimony.html.

65. *Barriers to Abortion are Barriers to Justice for Women*; available also at www.rcrc.org/pubs/speakout/barr.html.

66. Clergy for Choice Network pledge, cited in Clergy for Choice Network brochure; see also www.rcrc.org/clergy/clergy2.html.

67. See www.rcrc.org/rcrc/factsheet.html.

68. *Prayerfully Pro-Choice*, p. 64. All quotations in this and the following paragraph are from this litany.

69. *Prayerfully Pro-Choice*, p. 11; emphasis added.

70. A key article by Simmons, "Personhood, the Bible, and the Abortion Debate," may be found at www.rcrc.org/religion. Also there is an RCRC article with a similar thesis, "Is the Fetus a Person? The Bible's View," by Roy Bowen Ward.

71. See the same quote in the longer article, "Personhood, the Bible, and the Abortion Debate," at www.rcrc.org/religion/es3/bible2.html, under "The Biblical View of Person."

72. *Words of Choice: Countering Anti-Choice Rhetoric*, under "Human Being"; available also at www.rcrc.org/pubs/words.html.

73. *Prayerfully Pro-Choice*, p. 104.

74. *Words of Choice: Countering Anti-Choice Rhetoric*, under "Abortion for Convenience." See also the Alan Guttmacher Institute, *Facts in Brief: Induced Abortion* (New York: Alan Guttmacher Institute, 1996) and www.guttmacher.org/pubs/fb_induced_abortion.html (updated version). The Guttmacher Institute (named for Alan F. Guttmacher, President of Planned

Parenthood Federation of America in the late 1960s and early 1970s, but an independent organization), embraces a pro-choice perspective, but its statistics are generally accepted and used by people on all sides of the issue.

75. See www.guttmacher.org/pubs/fb_teen_sex.html (*Facts in Brief: Teen Sex and Pregnancy*), updated 1999.

76. See www.guttmacher.org/pubs/fb_induced_abortion.html (*Facts in Brief: Induced Abortion*). RCRC reports 58% (*Words of Choice: Countering Anti-Choice Rhetoric*, under "Abortion as Birth Control").

77. *Abortion and Women's Health* (New York: Alan Guttmacher Institute, 1990); details by age groups at: www.guttmacher.org/pubs/journals/2411798.html. More recent statistics are not available.

78. *Considering Abortion? Clarifying What You Believe*, p. 7.

79. *Prayerfully Pro-Choice*, p. 4.

80. *Prayerfully Pro-Choice*, p. 10.

81. *Prayerfully Pro-Choice*, p. 35.

82. *Prayerfully Pro-Choice*, p. 75. Neu is the co-founder and co-director of the Women's Alliance for Theology, Ethics and Ritual (WATER) She appears to be a Roman Catholic, at least in background. According to WATER's web site, Neu has three master's degrees from Roman Catholic institutions, and the majority of WATER's web site links are to organizations with a self-identified Catholic focus, including Catholics for a Free Choice. See www.his.com/~mhunt/diannneu.htm.

83. *Prayerfully Pro-Choice*, p. 80.

84. *Prayerfully Pro-Choice*, p. 82.

85. *Considering Abortion? Clarifying What You Believe*, p. 6. This does not mean that RCRC opposes late-term (post-"viability") abortions, for RCRC has consistently rejected all attempts to limit even "partial-birth" abortions.

86. *Prayerfully Pro-Choice*, p. 75.

87. *Prayerfully Pro-Choice*, p. 87.

88. *Prayerfully Pro-Choice*, p. 43.

89. *Prayerfully Pro-Choice*, p. 72.

90. *Prayerfully Pro-Choice*, p. 82.

91. *Prayerfully Pro-Choice*, p. 31.

92. *Prayerfully Pro-Choice*, p. 60.

93. *Prayerfully Pro-Choice*, p. 62.

94. *Prayerfully Pro-Choice*, p. 100.

95. *Prayerfully Pro-Choice*, p. 66.

96. "Prayer for Times of Decision: Affirming Women's Moral Agency," *Prayerfully Pro-Choice*, p. 4.

97. *Prayerfully Pro-Choice*, p. 2.

98. *Prayerfully Pro-Choice*, p. 83.

99. *Prayerfully Pro-Choice*, p. 35.

100. *Considering Abortion? Clarifying What You Believe*, p. 7. Since the name of Jesus seldom appears in RCRC literature, Jesus himself is not presented as pro-choice, though this conclusion has been drawn by others. In a letter responding to an edition of "The O'Reilly Factor" (Fox News Channel, Nov. 19, 2002) that criticized Planned Parenthood's 2002 holiday card, "Choice on Earth," United Church of Christ minister Rev. Mark Bigelow (a member of Planned Parenthood's Clergy Advisory Board) said the following: "In your show you said that Jesus was not pro-choice and you were sure he would be insulted were he to see this card. Even as a minister I am careful what I presume Jesus would do if he were alive today, but *one thing I know from the Bible is that Jesus was not against women having a choice in continuing a pregnancy*. He never said a word about abortion (nor did anyone else in the Bible) even though abortion was available and in use in his time. In addition, his compassionate stance toward all individuals causes me to believe that he would want us to do what we can to ensure that women have full access to all necessary medical care in order to have healthy and happy families. *Jesus was for peace on earth, justice on earth, compassion on earth, mercy on earth, and choice on earth.*"

See www.ppfa.org/about/pr/021126_gloria_letter.html#mark for this statement. For the anti-abortion position of first-century Jews, see section IV.6 below, "The Character of the God Attested in Scripture."

101. In certain parts of the New Testament, such as the book of Revelation, the language of holy warfare is maintained but the reality completely transformed. In Revelation, for instance, no human being fights for God in the ultimate triumph of justice over evil; in fact, the divine victory is accomplished, ironically, not by literal warfare but through the death and the word of the lamb who was slain.

102. This commitment was reaffirmed by the General Synod of the United Church of Christ in 1991; by the 71st General Convention of the Episcopal Church in 1994; by the General Conference of The United Methodist Church in 1996; and by the 204th General Assembly of the Presbyterian Church (USA) in 1997.

103. F. Forrester Church, "A Just-War Theory for Abortion," *The Christian Century*, Aug. 26–Sept. 2, 1987: 733-34. Already in 1976 The American Lutheran Church had received a study document by James H. Burtness proposing a "theory of justified abortion" modeled on the just-war tradition ("A Statement on Abortion," section 4, "Parameters for Reflection"; see www.elca.org/jle/alc/alc. value_human_life_part2.html).

104. Gabriel Fackre and Dorothy Ashman Fackre, "Abortion," in James W. Cox, ed., *Handbook of Themes for Preaching* (Louisville: Westminster John Knox, 1991), pp. 23-27. See also the careful, extended argument of another UCC theologian in Lloyd Steffen, *Life Choice: The Theory of Just Abortion* (Cleveland: Pilgrim, 1994).

105. Even Rev. Howard Moody finds parallels between abortion and war, hinting at the necessity for criteria (*Prayerfully Pro-Choice*, pp. 7-8). However, he makes two major errors: he assumes that the fetus is always an "enemy"

about which a decision must be made regarding lethal force, and he abandons the attempt to establish criteria for a justifiable abortion because, as in warfare, there are conflicting views about when the use of force might be ethical.

106. "UMC Actions and Reactions," *The Christian Century* June 3-10, 1992, pp. 575-76, and www.umc.org/judicial/600/683.html (the judicial ruling).

107. "Responsible Parenthood," first adopted in 1976 and amended and re-adopted in 1996 (*The Book of Resolutions of The United Methodist Church — 2000*, res. 22, pp. 121-24).

108. See www.umc-gbcs.org/csamay2_june2002.htm.

109. The core of the church's statement on abortion dates from 1972, when it called for the "removal of abortion from the criminal code" but also expressed its belief in "the sanctity of unborn human life" and its reluctance to "approve abortion" (*The Book of Discipline of The United Methodist Church — 1972*, para. 72D). For a helpful history of the statement's development, see http://umns.umc.org/backgrounders/abortion.html.

110. This clause was added in 1988 (*The Book of Discipline of The United Methodist Church — 1988*, para. 71G).

111. This clause was introduced in 1992 (*The Book of Discipline of The United Methodist Church — 1992*, para. 71H) but did not originally mention those in the midst of a crisis pregnancy; that was added in 1996.

112. *The Book of Discipline of The United Methodist Church – 2000*, para. 161J (The United Methodist Publishing House, 2000). The statement is supplemented with practical and legal guidelines in resolution 22, "Responsible Parenthood," noted above.

113. *The Book of Discipline of The United Methodist Church – 2000*, para. 164G.

114. *The Book of Discipline of The United Methodist Church – 2000*, para. 161G.

115. See www.pcusa.org/paro/who.html.

116. Minutes of the 204th General Assembly (1992), Presbyterian Church (USA).

117. Minutes of the 209th General Assembly (1997), Presbyterian Church (USA).

118. Minutes of the 214th General Assembly (2002), Presbyterian Church (USA).

119. Second Helvetic Confession, chap. 29 = *The Book of Confessions*, Article 5.251; *The Confession of 1967* II.A.4.d = *The Book of Confessions* Article 9.47. These may be found online at www.pcusa.org. This tradition was recently reaffirmed (in 2001) by Rev. Clifton Kirkpatrick, the denomination's Stated Clerk. See the report from the Presbyterian News Service at www.pcusa.org/pcnews/oldnews/2001/01108.htm, p. 2.

120. Overture 98-45; see www.wfn.org/1998/09/msg00129.html.

121. General Convention, *Journal of the General Convention of...The Episcopal Church, 1994* (New York: General Convention, 1995), pp. 323-25 (res. 1994-A054). This and other documents may be accessed online at www.episcopalchurch.org/gc/cc/default.htm. The "unequivocal opposition" paragraph had been struck from the original resolution in 1988, according to a report in *Christianity Today*, Sept. 2, 1988, p. 48.

122. General Convention, *Journal of the General Convention of...The Episcopal Church, 1994* (New York: General Convention, 1995), pp. 323-25 (res. 1994-A054).

123. General Convention, *Journal of the General Convention of...The Episcopal Church, 1982* (New York: General Convention, 1983), p. C-157 (res. 1982-065).

124. General Convention, *Journal of the General Convention of...The Episcopal Church, 1994* (New York: General Convention, 1995), p. 325 (res. 1994-D-105).

125. *Words of Choice: Countering Anti-Choice Rhetoric*, under "Crisis Pregnancy Counseling Centers."

126. 73rd General Convention, 2000; this recent text related to abortion may be viewed at www.episcopalchurch.org/gc/hd/ResolutionsToDioceses.pdf (res. 2000-D083).

127. General Convention, *Journal of the General Convention of...The Episcopal Church, 1997* (New York: General Convention, 1998), p. 270 (res. 1997-D065s).

128. General Convention, *Journal of the General Convention of...The Episcopal Church, 1997* (New York: General Convention, 1998), p. 277 (res. 1997-D032a).

129. See www.ekk.org/resoluti.htm.

130. This statement is not currently on the UCC site (www.ucc.org), but it may be found on the RCRC site at www.rcrc.org/religion/weaffirm/affirm.html#ucc.

131. This and the following quotations come from the 1987 statement, "Sexuality and Abortion: A Faithful Response."

132. See, for example, the story in *Time*, July 4, 1988, p. 44.

133. See www.abc-usa.org/resources/resol/abortion.htm.

134. *Resolutions and Elections of the Provincial Synod of the Northern Province of the Moravian Church 1986*, pp. 35-36. See www.moravian.org/faq/abortion.html.

135. *Resolutions and Elections of the Provincial Synod of the Northern Province of the Moravian Church 1990*, p. 46.

136. *Resolutions and Elections of the Provincial Synod of the Northern Province of the Moravian Church 1986*, pp. 35-36.

137. *Resolutions and Elections of the Provincial Synod of the Northern Province of the Moravian Church 1974*, pp. 55-57.

138. *Resolutions and Elections of the Provincial Synod of the Northern Province of the Moravian Church 1990*, p. 46.

139. Personal correspondence from Joel Thoreson, Reference Archivist, the Evangelical Lutheran Church in America, November 19, 2002.

140. Second biennial Churchwide Assembly of the Evangelical Lutheran Church in America, 1991, *A Social Statement on Abortion*; www.elca.org/dcs/abortion.html. This excerpt and those that follow may be found in the statement at this web site.

141. *A Social Statement on Abortion*, addendum A.

142. *A Message on Sexuality: Some Common Convictions*; www.elca.org/dcs/sexuality.html; p. 4. In this report, the ELCA, like the PC(USA), views marriage as a "lifelong covenant of faithfulness between a man and a woman" within which responsible procreation and parenting may occur (p. 3). It also describes promiscuity ("[h]aving casual sexual relations") as *"inconsistent with our identity as Christians"* (p. 5). Therefore, said the ELCA, "we affirm the importance of education about sexuality that emphasizes respect, mutuality, responsibility, and *abstinence outside of marriage*" (p. 5).

143. *A Social Statement on Abortion*, section V.C.

144. Leonard R. Klein, "Abortion: The Crisis in the Churches," pp. 17-35 in Paul T. Stallsworth, ed., *Thinking Theologically about Abortion* (Anderson, Ind.: Bristol House, 2000), p. 18.

145. Karl Barth, *Karl Barth's Table Talk* (Atlanta: John Knox, 1963), p. 37.

146. Gerald Bonner, "Abortion and Early Christian Thought," pp. 93-122 in J.H. Channer, ed., *Abortion and the Sanctity of Human Life* (Exeter: Paternoster; Greenwood, S.C.: Attic,1985) p. 111. See also Michael J. Gorman, "Ahead to Our Past: Abortion and Early Christian Texts," pp. 25-43 in Stallsworth, *The Church and Abortion*, pp. 29-30, 37.

147. Pope John Paul II, *The Gospel of Life [Evangelium Vitae]* (New York: Random House, 1995), para. 12; cf. para. 23-24, 28.

148. Gorman, "Ahead to Our Past: Abortion and Early Christian Texts," p. 28.

149. Terry Schlossberg and Elizabeth Achtemeier, *Not My Own: Abortion and the Marks of the Church* (Grand Rapids: Eerdmans, 1995), p. 17.

150. Schlossberg and Achtemeier, *Not My Own*, p. 16.

151. Schlossberg and Achtemeier, *Not My Own*, pp. 26-27.

152. Church, "A Just-War Theory for Abortion," p. 734.

153. Gorman, "Ahead to Our Past: Abortion and Early Christian Texts," p. 37.

154. J.W. Rogerson, "Using the Bible in the Debate about Abortion," pp. 77-92 in Channer, *Abortion and the Sanctity of Human Life*, here pp. 89-90.

155. In "An Account of the Conference Conversation," in Stallsworth, *The Church and Abortion*, p. 118.

156. Stanley Hauerwas, "Abortion, Theologically Understood," pp. 44-66 in Stallsworth, *The Church and Abortion*, here p. 55.

157. She is quoted in Hauerwas, "Abortion, Theologically Understood," p. 47.

158. Hauerwas, "Abortion, Theologically Understood," pp. 49-50.

159. Schlossberg and Achtemeier, *Not My Own*, p. 43.

160. Gorman, "Ahead to Our Past," p. 37.

161. *We Remember*, p. 3.

162. Richard B. Hays, *The Moral Vision of the New Testament: A Contemporary Introduction to New Testament Ethics* (San Francisco: HarperSanFrancisco, 1996), p. 452; emphasis his.

163. Hays, *The Moral Vision of the New Testament*, p. 452; emphasis his.

164. O.M.T. O'Donovan, "Again: Who is a Person?" in Channer, *Abortion and the Sanctity of Human Life*, pp. 125-137.

165. Hays, *The Moral Vision of the New Testament*, p. 451; emphasis his.

166. See Bonner, "Abortion and Early Christian Thought" and Michael J. Gorman, *Abortion and the Early Church: Christian, Pagan, and Jewish Attitudes in the Greco-Roman World* (Downers Grove, Ill.: InterVarsity and Mahwah, N.J.: Paulist, 1982; repr. Eugene, Ore.: Wipf & Stock, 1998), especially pp. 47-73.

167. See the text of this document at either www.linacre.org/atheol.html; www.ethicsandmedicine.com/17/3/17-3-jones.htm; or *Ethics & Medicine: An International Journal of Bioethics* 17:3 (Fall 2001): 143-54.

168. The principal author was *Rev. David Jones*, Director of the Linacre Centre for Healthcare Ethics, London. The complete list of signers, in alphabetical order, follows: *Cardinal Cahal B. Daly*, Peritus at Vatican II, Archbishop Emeritus of Armagh, and Primate Emeritus of All Ireland; *Rt. Rev. Kallistos Ware*, Bishop of Diokleia in the Orthodox Archdiocese of Thyateira and Great Britain, and Lecturer in Eastern Orthodox Studies, Oxford University; *Most Rev. Rowan Williams*, then Bishop of Monmouth and Archbishop of Wales, formerly Lady Margaret Professor of Divinity of Oxford, and now Archbishop of Canterbury; *Rev. Prof. Benedict M. Ashley*, Adjunct Professor, Center for Healthcare Ethics, St Louis University, St Louis, Missouri; *Dr. Margaret Atkins*, Lecturer in Theology, Trinity and All Saints College, Leeds; *Rev. Prof. Michael Banner*, Professor of Moral and Social Theology, King's College, London; *Rev. Prof. Nigel M. de S. Cameron*, Professor of Theology and Culture, Trinity International University, Illinois; *Prof. Celia Deane-Drummond*, Professor in Theology and the Biological Sciences, Chester College, University of Liverpool; *Prof. Vigen Guroian*, Professor of Theology and Ethics, Loyola College, Baltimore, Maryland, and Visiting Lecturer, St. Nersess Armenian Seminary; *Prof. Andrew Louth*, Professor of Patristic and Byzantine Studies, University of Durham; *Prof. William E. May*, Professor of Moral Theology, John Paul II Institute for Marriage and Family, Washington, D.C.; *Rev. Herbert McCabe*, Lecturer in Theology, Blackfriars Hall, Oxford; *Prof. Gilbert Meilaender*, Professor of Christian Ethics, Valparaiso University, Indiana; *Prof. John Milbank*, Professor of Philosophical Theology, University of Virginia; *Dr. C. Ben Mitchell*, Senior Fellow, The Center for Bioethics & Human Dignity, Bannockburn, Illinois; *Rev. Dr. Aidan Nichols*, Affiliated Lecturer, Divinity Faculty, Cambridge University, and Lecturer in Theology, Blackfriars Hall, Oxford; *Rev. Prof. Oliver O'Donovan*, Canon of Christ Church and Regius

Professor of Moral and Pastoral Theology, Oxford University; *Rev. Terence Phipps*, Lecturer in Moral Theology, Allen Hall, London; *Prof. John Rist*, Professor Emeritus, University of Toronto, and Visiting Professor, Institutum Patristicum Augustinianum, Rome; *Prof. John Saward*, Professor of Dogmatic Theology, International Theological Institute, Gaming, Austria, and Aquinas Fellow, Plater College, Oxford; *Dr. Robert Song*, Lecturer in Theology, University of Durham; *Rev. Dr. Thomas G. Weinandy*, Warden, Tutorial Fellow in Theology, Greyfriars, Oxford; and one of the present writers (*Gorman*).

169. See www.spuc.org.uk/releases/20020723.htm.

170. Rowan Williams, then Bishop of Monmouth, in a 1999 interview (www.prayerbook.ca/cann/1999/03/pblam110.htm), p. 7, quoting in part a sermon from his book *Open to Judgement: Sermons and Addresses* (London: Darton, Longman & Todd, 1994).

171. Jürgen Moltmann, *The Way of Jesus Christ: Christology in Messianic Dimensions*; trans. Margaret Kohl (New York: HarperCollins, 1990), p. 268.

172. Dietrich Bonhoeffer, *Ethics* (trans. N. H. Smith; New York: Macmillan, 1955), p. 131.

173. Rogerson, "Using the Bible in the Debate about Abortion," p. 91.

174. Rogerson, "Using the Bible in the Debate about Abortion," pp. 80-81.

175. See, e.g., Robert M. Grant, *Paul in the Roman World: The Conflict at Corinth* (Louisville: Westminster John Knox, 2001), pp. 112-13; Thomas Wiedenmann, *Adults and Children in the Roman Empire* (New Haven: Yale University Press, 1989), p. 37; John M.G. Barclay, *Jews in the Mediterranean Diaspora From Alexander to Trajan (323 BCE - 117 CE)* (Edinburgh: T&T Clark, 1996), pp. 428-29; Bonner, "Abortion and Early Christian Thought," pp. 100-103; and Gorman, *Abortion and the Early Church*, pp. 33-45.

176. Bonner, "Abortion and Early Christian Thought," p. 94. See also Gorman, *Abortion and the Early Church*.

177. For this argument, see Michael J. Gorman, "Why is the New Testament Silent about Abortion?", *Christianity Today* 37/1 (Jan. 11, 1993): 27-29. For a critique by Paul Simmons (who has written significant pieces for RCRC) as well as a response to his critique, see Paul D. Simmons, "Biblical Authority and the Not-So Strange Silence of Scripture about Abortion (*Christian Bioethics* 2 [1996]: 66-82) and Michael J. Gorman, "Scripture, History, and Authority in a Christian View of Abortion: A Response to Paul Simmons" (*Christian Bioethics* 2 [1996]: 83-96).

178. Hays, *The Moral Vision of the New Testament*, p. 450; emphasis his.

179. Church of the Brethren, 1984 Report from the General Board, Statement on Abortion, at www.brethren.org/ac/ac_statements/84Abortion.htm.

www.ingramcontent.com/pod-product-compliance
Lightning Source LLC
LaVergne TN
LVHW021617080426
835510LV00019B/2621